Thesaurus

Compiled by Fran Pickering
Illustrated by Helen Marsden,
Dave Farris, Pat McCarthy,
Heather Clarke, Ian Briars

HENDERSON
PUBLISHING PLC

INTRODUCTION

1. This book is arranged alphabetically, like a dictionary. Each word is called an 'entry'.

2. Each entry is numbered.

3. Next to each entry is an abbreviation to show whether the word is a noun, verb, adjective, etc.

Abbreviations:

adj.	adjective
adv.	adverb
conj.	conjunction
n.	noun
n.pl.	plural noun
prep.	preposition
pron.	pronoun
v.	verb

4. Following each numbered word are a few synonyms: words that have a similar meaning to the numbered word.

5. After that some antonyms are shown. An antonym is a word that has the opposite meaning to the entry. 'A' = Antonym.

6. Where relevant the book also shows homonyms. A homonym is a word which is either spelt the same or sounds the same as the entry word, but has a different meaning e.g. 'aisle' and 'isle'. 'H' = Homonym.

7. Some entries have related words shown in brackets at the end of the entry e.g. apathy (apathetic).

A1. abandon. v.
1. leave, cancel, discard
2. desert, forsake
3. maroon n. freedom, recklessness, enthusiasm (the girl danced with abandon).
A: 1. continue, maintain.

A2. ability. n. skill, aptitude, capacity. A: inability, incompetence.

A3. able. adj.
1. capable, fit, qualified
2. allowed, free to.
A: 1. incapable, unqualified
2. not free (I am unable to come because I have a previous engagement).

A4. above. adv.
1. overhead, higher than, more than
2. superior. A: 1. below, lower than 2. inferior.

A5. abrupt. adj. sudden, hasty, curt. A: gradual, easy, gracious.

A6. accept. v. receive, admit, acknowledge.
A: refuse, deny, disown.

A7. access. n. entrance, way in, approach, admission.
A: exit.

A8. account. n.
1. report, story
2. financial record
3. worth, significance.

A9. accurate. adj. exact, precise, correct.
A: wrong, careless.

A10. achieve. v. attain, reach, finish.
A: neglect, fail.

A11. acknowledge. v.
1. recognise, accept
2. respond to, answer.
A: 1. disclaim, reject
2. ignore.

A12. acquire. v. get, obtain. A: lose, give up.

A

A13. act. v. behave, perform n. 1. deed, performance 2. pretence 3. law. A: v. procrastinate, to put off, stop.

A14. active. adj. 1. agile, energetic 2. busy. A: inactive.

A15. actual. adj. real, true, genuine, certain. A: nonexistent, probable, fictitious.

A16. adjust. v. 1. alter, regulate, fix, change 2. get used to, adapt to.

A17. admit. v. 1. confess 2. let in 3. permit. A: 1. deny 2. exclude 3. forbid.

A18. adore. v. love, cherish, worship. A: hate, loathe, dislike.

A19. advance. v. 1. go forward, proceed, approach, continue 2. suggest, propose n. progress. A: 1. retreat, regress 2. withhold, suppress n. retrogression.

A20. advantage. n. benefit, gain, favour. A: disadvantage, hindrance.

A21. advice. n. guidance, counsel, suggestion.

A22. affect. v. influence, alter.

A23. affection. n. liking, warmth, tenderness, fondness. A: coolness, disinterest.

A24. afraid. adj. scared, fearful, frightened. A: fearless, bold.

A25. after. prep. following, behind, later. A: before.

A26. age. n. 1. period, era, time 2. seniority, adulthood v. mature, ripen, grow old. A: 1. instant, second 2. childhood.

A27. aged. adj. old, elderly, ancient.
A: young.

A28. aggravate. v.
1. make worse, intensify, exaggerate 2. irritate, annoy. A: 1. improve, relieve 2. soothe, calm.

A29. aggressive. adj. belligerent, hostile, pugnacious, forceful.
A: peaceful, friendly, submissive, shy.

A30. agile. adj. nimble, lithe, supple, dexterous.
A: clumsy, awkward, sluggish, lethargic.

A31. agony. n.
torment, anguish, misery, suffering.
A: pleasure, ease, comfort.

A32. agree. v. assent, consent, concur, match.
A: disagree, dispute, oppose, contradict.

A33. agreeable. adj. pleasing, gratifying, consenting, friendly
A: displeasing, unpleasant, offensive, disapproving.

A34. aid. v.
help, assist, support
n. assistance, charity.
A: harm, hinder, thwart.

A35. aim. v.
1. point, direct
2. try, intend, work toward
3. n. purpose, goal, plan.

A36. air. n.
1. atmosphere
2. breeze, draught
3. manner, style
4. affectedness, pretence, arrogance
5. tune, melody, song
v. 1. ventilate, expose to air 2. tell, express, disclose (she aired her views).

A37. aisle. n. passage, corridor, gangway. H: isle.

A38. alarm. v. frighten, scare, startle n. 1. signal, siren apprehension, dismay, fear. A: assure v. 1. all clear 2. composure.

A39. alert. adj. aware, observant, attentive v. warn, caution. A: adj. dull, unaware v. lull.

A40. allow. v. permit, let, go along with, give A: forbid, refuse.

A41. alone. adv. separately, unaided adj. single, solitary, isolated, unique, forsaken. A: adv. jointly, assisted adj. together with.

A42. already. adj. by this time, yet, previously.

A43. alter. v. change, vary, modify, amend. A: keep, retain.

A44. altogether. adv. completely, entirely, as a whole, collectively. A: partially, separately.

A45. always. adv. forever, eternally. A: never.

A46. amaze. v. astonish, astound, surprise. A: expect.

A47. amiable. adj. friendly, good-natured, kindly. A: unfriendly, disagreeable.

A48. ample. adj. enough, sufficient, abundant, plentiful. A: insufficient, scant, little.

A49. amuse. v. entertain, divert, occupy, delight. A: bore, annoy.

A50. ancient. adj.
archaic, antique, aged,
long past.
A: recent, new.

A51. anger. n. rage,
fury, wrath, temper
v. infuriate, madden,
enrage.
A: n. calmness, goodwill
v. placate, soothe.

A52. anguish. n.
distress, misery,
heartache, grief.
A: comfort, consolation,
relief.

A53. announce. v.
declare, state, proclaim,
broadcast, publish.
A: suppress, conceal.

A54. annoy. v. irritate,
bother, pester,
exasperate.
A: please, calm.

A55. answer. v.
reply, respond
n. solution, explanation,
response.
A: v. question, query.

A56. anticipate. v.
expect, await, look
forward to.
A: dread, doubt.

A57. anxiety. n. worry,
apprehension, unease.
A: assurance, relief,
confidence.

A58. apparent. adj.
obvious, evident, plain,
clear.
A: hidden, mysterious.

A59. appeal. v.
1. plead, beg, implore
2. attract, allure,
fascinate n. 1. request,
petition 2. attraction,
fascination. A: v. 2. repel
n. 1. refusal, rejection .

A60 . appear. v.
1. show up, emerge
2. seem, look.
A: 1. disappear
2. be unclear.

A61. applaud. v.
clap, praise, commend
A: boo, criticise.

A

A62. apply. v. 1. put on 2. use, employ 3. be applicable 4. request (apply for a job) 5. devote, dedicate (apply to the task).

A63. appreciation. n. 1. gratitude 2. understanding 3. increase in value. A: 1. ingratitude 2. ignorance, aversion 3. devaluation.

A64. apprehend. v. 1. arrest, capture 2. understand, realise. A: 1. release 2. misunderstand.

A65. approve. v. 1. like, appreciate 2. permit, allow 3. endorse, authorise. A: 1. disapprove, dislike 2. disallow 3. reject.

A 66. arduous. adj. difficult, hard, laborious. A: easy.

A67. area. n. region, extent, portion, territory.

A68. argue. v. discuss, debate, disagree, quarrel. A: agree.

A69. aroma. n. good smell, scent, fragrance. A: stink, stench.

A70. arrange. v. 1. order, organise, group 2. plan, prepare. A: 1. disarrange.

A71. arrest. v. 1. capture, apprehend, seize 2. stop, stay. A: 1. release 2. encourage.

A72. arrive. v. 1. come, reach, appear, turn up 2. succeed. A: 1. depart, withdraw 2. fail.

A73. arrogant. adj. proud, haughty, conceited. A: unassuming, polite, modest.

A74. artificial. adj.
false, man-made, faked,
unnatural.
A: natural, genuine,
sincere, authentic.

A75. ask. v. request,
question, inquire.
A: give, answer, inform.

A76. assemble. v.
1. meet, congregate
2. gather, collect 3. put
together, build, join.
A: 1. disband, adjourn
2. disperse, distribute
3. knock down, demolish.

A77. assent. v. agree,
consent, approve.
A: dissent, disagree, refuse.

A78. assess. v. look
over, appraise, estimate.

A79. asset. n.
advantage, benefit,
resource. A: liability,
handicap, debt.

A80. assist. v. help,
aid, support, serve.
A: hinder, impede,
oppose.

A81. assume. v.
1. suppose, guess,
presume, suspect 2. take
on, adopt, take over.

A82. assure. v.
promise, pledge,
guarantee, convince.
A: deny, refute, lie.

A83. astonish. v.
surprise, astound, amaze.
A: anticipate, bore.

A84. attach. v. fasten,
join, connect, fix.
A: detach, disconnect.

A85. attain. v. achieve,
gain, reach, accomplish.
A: lose, give up, fail.

A86. attempt. v.
try, make an effort,
have a go, endeavour.

A

A87. attitude. n.
1. posture, stance, pose
2. frame of mind, manner.

A88. attract. v. draw, lure, appeal to, entice. A: repel, repulse.

A89. authentic. adj. genuine, real, true, actual.
A: imitation, fake, sham.

A90. automatic. adj.
1. involuntary, spontaneous, reflex
2. mechanical, programmed.
A: 1. conscious, intentional 2. manual.

A91. average. adj.
1. common, typical, usual 2. middle, medium.
A: 1. unusual 2. extreme.

A92. aversion. n. disgust, dislike, revulsion, distaste. A: love, inclination, desire.

A93. avert. v. turn away, prevent, avoid, ward off. A: invite.

A94. avid. adj. eager, enthusiastic, greedy. A: indifferent.

A95. avoid. v. evade, dodge, keep clear of. A: seek, meet, face, confront.

A96. award. v. give, grant, bestow, present n. prize, trophy. A: v. withhold, deny.

A97. aware. adj. conscious, observant, knowledgeable. A: unaware, oblivious, ignorant.

A98. awry. adj. adv. askew, crooked, twisted; wrong, amiss. A: straight, even, right.

B1. back. n. spine, end, rear, reverse 1. v. move away, retreat
2. support, promote.
A: n. front v.1. move toward 2. oppose.

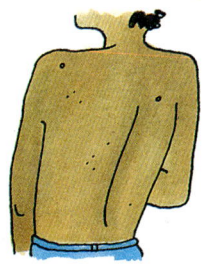

B2 background. n.
1. setting, distance, landscape 2. experience, upbringing, environment.
A:1. foreground 2. future.

B3 bad. adj.
1. inferior, defective
2. immoral, sinful
3. awful, appalling
4. harmful, hurtful
5. spoiled, rotten, tainted
6. disagreeable, unpleasant 7. ill, unwell
A:1. superior 2. virtuous, moral 6. agreeable, beneficial, pleasant
7. well.

B4 baffle. v.
1. deaden, muffle (noise)
2. confuse, bewilder.
A: 1. admit, transmit
2. explain to.

B5 bail. n. bond, surety v. ladle, scoop.
H: bale.

B6 bale. n. bundle, parcel, truss, load.
H: bail.

B7 baleful. adj. sinister, threatening, ominous.
A: friendly, kindly.

B8 balmy. adj.
1. gentle, mild, soft
2. fragrant, sweet-smelling. A:1. harsh, intense, rough 2. foul, smelly.

B9 ban. v. forbid, prohibit, bar
n. restriction, veto.
A: v. allow, authorise
n. authorisation.

B10 banal. adj. trite, commonplace, ordinary.
A: original, new, exciting.

B11 band. n.
1. group, company, troop 2. belt, loop, strip.

B

B12 banish. v. exile, cast out, ban, shut out, drive away. A: invite, accept, welcome.

B13 bar. n. 1. rod, pole 2. block, ingot 3. sandbar, shoal, bank 4. serving counter, pub, sandwich bar 5. group of lawyers 6. court, tribunal 7. barrier, obstacle 8. ban, prohibition 9. band, strip 10. measure of time in music. v. prohibit

B14 bargain. n. 1. agreement, contract, deal 2. good buy v. negotiate, haggle. A: 2. extravagance v. swindle.

B15 base. n. 1. bottom, stand, foundation 2. station, headquarters v. establish, place adj. 1. inferior, poor quality 2. low, vile, mean. A: adj. 1. precious, valuable 2. honourable, good, upright.

B16 basic. adj. fundamental, essential, core.

B17 bay. n. 1. cove, inlet 2. alcove, recess 3. cornered, trapped (animal at bay) v. bark, howl.

B18 beam. n. 1. rafter, joist, timber 2. ray, shaft, glow v. 1. transmit, emit, radiate 2. smile, shine.

B19 beat. v. 1. hit, strike 2. mix, stir 3. defeat, overcome 4. throb, pulsate. A: 1. stroke, caress 3. lose, surrender.

B20 beg. v. 1. ask, plead, implore 2. evade, avoid, dodge (your reply begs the question).

B21 begin. v. start, commence, initiate. A: end, finish, terminate.

B22 begrudge. v.
envy, resent.

B23 behaviour. n.
conduct, manner,
attitude.

B24 behold. v.
see, notice, observe.

B25 being. n.
1. existence, reality
2. living creature 3. soul,
spirit. A: 1. nothingness.

B26 bellow. v. roar,
shout. A: whisper.

B27 below. adv.
1. under, beneath
2. prep. less than.
A: 1. above
2. greater than.

B28 beneficial. adj.
useful, favourable,
helpful.
A: useless, harmful.

B29 benefit. n.
1. help, asset
2. charity performance
v. help, aid, assist.
A: 1.damage, harm, loss.

B30 benevolent. adj.
kindhearted, generous,
considerate. A: unkind,
selfish, malicious.

B31 bent. adj.
angled, curved, crooked
n. tendency, leaning,
inclination. A: adj.
straight n. aversion.

B32 beseech. v. beg,
plead with, appeal to.

B33 best. adj. most
excellent, superior, top,
finest. A: worst.

B34 bet. v. n. wager,
gamble, stake.

B35 better. adj.
1. superior, preferable
2. improved 3. greater,
larger (better part of)
v. improve, upgrade.
A: 1. inferior 2. worse
3. lesser v. worsen.

B36 beware. v. look
out, take warning, be
careful, guard against.

B

B37 bewilder. v.
confuse, baffle, puzzle,
mystify.
A: enlighten, inform.

B38 bewitch. v.
enchant, entrance,
captivate, fascinate.
A: repel.

B39 beyond. prep.
past, farther on than.
A: beside, here.

B40 bicker. v. argue,
squabble, disagree,
quarrel. A: agree.

B41 bid. v.
1. command, order
2. tell, say 3. offer.
A: 1. forbid.

B42 big. adj. 1. large,
huge, enormous
2. important, major
3. generous,
magnanimous (big heart)
4. grown-up 5. boastful,
conceited (big talk).
A: 1. little, small
2. unimportant,
insignificant 3. mean,
unjust 4. young
5. humble, modest.

B43 bigotry. n.
intolerance, prejudice,
narrow-mindedness.
A: tolerance.

B44 bill. n. 1. invoice,
account 2. banknote
3. law, act 4. poster,
notice, advertisement,
5. programme, agenda.

B45 bind. v.
1. tie up, fasten, secure
2. bandage, wrap
3. require, oblige (the
contract binds) 4. trim,
edge. A: 1.untie, free
2. unwrap 3. exempt.

B46 bit. n. 1. small
piece, fragment, trace
2. harness.

B47 biting. adj.
1. stinging, cutting,
piercing 2. sarcastic,
caustic. A: 1. mild
2. pleasant, genial.

B48 bitter. adj.
1. sour, tart (taste);
2. acrid (smell)
3. cold, severe (weather)
4. resentful, angry, jealous (feelings)
5. distressing, painful (experience)
A: 1,2. sweet, cloying
3. balmy 4. grateful, appreciative 5. joyful.

B49 bizarre. adj.
fantastic, weird, strange, unusual. A: ordinary.

B50 blame. v.
accuse, charge, condemn, rebuke
n. responsibility, guilt.
A: v. clear, absolve, excuse, vindicate
n. acclaim, praise.

B51 bland. adj.
uninteresting, dull, uninspiring.
A: exciting, stirring.

B52 blank. adj.
1. unmarked, unused
2. vacant, empty (blank gaze). A: 1. marked, full
2. expressive.

B53 blast. n. 1. gust, gale (of air) 2. explosion, boom 3. loud noise, blare.

B54 bleak. adj. bare, barren, desolate.
A: cheerful, wooded.

B55 blend. v. mix, combine, merge.
A: separate, clash.

B56 bless. v.
1. dedicate, make holy
2. approve, favour, sanction. A: curse

B57 bliss. n. joy, delight, happiness, glee.
A: misery, sorrow.

B58 blot. n. 1. spot, blemish, mark, stain
2. conceal, cover, erase (blot out).

B59 blow. n. 1. hit, knock, punch 2. shock, misfortune v. 1. exhale, puff 2. sound, play (blow your horn) 3. burst, explode (blow a fuse).
A: 1. caress 2. blessing
v.1. inhale.

B

B60. bluff. v.
deceive, pretend, fake.

B61. blurred. adj.
unclear, fuzzy, misty.
A: clear.

B62. boast. v.
brag, crow, swank, gloat.
A: disclaim.

B63. body. n.
1. person, being 2. the
main part 3. group,
party, mass. A: 1. soul,
spirit 2. minority 3. few.

B64. bold. adj.
1. brave, adventurous,
daring 2. rude,
impudent, brazen.
A: 1. fearful 2. shy.

B65. bolt. n.
1. bar, catch, lock
2. dash, rush v.1. flee,
run 2. gobble, gulp.

B66. bonus. n. reward,
gift, premium, extra.
A: penalty.

B67. bore. v. 1. drill,
pierce 2. tire, weary.
A: 1. fill, plug 2. interest,
excite.

B68. borrow. v. take
on loan, use. A: lend.

B69. bother. v.
1. upset, pester, harass
2. care, mind
n. 1. trouble, incon-
venience, nuisance
2. commotion, disturbance.
A: 1. help, aid
2. neglect.

B70. boundless. adj.
endless, everlasting,
limitless, unrestricted.
A: limited, bounded.

B71. box. n.
carton, crate, case
v. cuff, slap, hit.

B72. bracing. adj.
stimulating, refreshing,
invigorating.
A: soporific, depressing.

B73. brag. v.
boast, swank, talk big.

B74. branch. n.
1. section, department
2. bough, limb (tree).
A: 1. main office
2. trunk.

B75. brand. n.
1. type, make, trademark
2. mark, stamp.

B76. brawl. n. fight, scuffle, rumpus, fracas.

B77. brazen. adj. shameless, bold, immodest, brash. A: reserved, timid.

B78. breathtaking. adj. awesome, exciting, amazing.

B79. breed. v. reproduce, multiply, increase n. species, kind, type. A: v. destroy, wipe out.

B80. bribe. v.
1. buy off, entice
2. n. hush money.

B81. brief. adj.
1. short-lived, momentary, hasty (brief pause) 2. concise, short, terse (brief outline). A: 1. lengthy (brevity).

B82. bright. adj.
1. brilliant, dazzling, vivid
2. cheerful, lively, gay
3. clever, brainy, intelligent. A: 1. drab, dull 2. glum, forlorn
3. stupid, simple.

B83. brim. n. rim, upper edge, brink.

B84. brisk. adj. energetic, vigorous, quick, spry. A: sluggish, lethargic, lazy.

B85. brittle. adj. breakable, fragile. A: resilient, sturdy.

B86. broad. adj. wide, extensive, outspread. A: narrow.

B87. broadcast. v. transmit, send out, announce, disperse.

B88. broken. adj.
fractured, fragmented,
smashed, damaged.
A: whole.

B89. brunt. n.
full force, main shock,
impact.

B90. brutal. adj. cruel,
vicious, savage, pitiless.
A: humane, merciful.

B91. budge. v. move,
shift. A: remain, stay.

B92. bulge. n.
1. lump, bump, hump
v. swell, protrude, stick
out. A: n. hollow
v. shrink.

B93. bulk. n. mass,
size, hugeness, magnitude
A: smallest part.

B94. bulletin. n. news
report, announcement,
notice, dispatch.

B95. bundle. n.
parcel, package, bale,
packet v. tie together,
wrap. A: v. disperse.

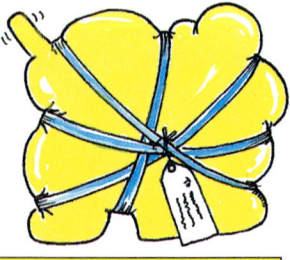

B96. bungle. v.
blunder, botch, do badly,
make a mess of.

B97. buoyant. adj.
1. light, floatable
2. cheerful, lighthearted.

B98. burly. adj. sturdy,
muscular, brawny.
A: puny, weak.

B99. burnish. v.
polish, shine, buff.

B100. burst. v.
explode, shatter,
fragment, fly apart.
A: hold together, join.

B101. bury. v. inter,
entomb, conceal, cover.
A: unearth, reveal.

B102. busy. adj.
occupied, active,
employed. A: idle.

B103. butt. n.
1. blunt end, stump
2. target, victim (butt of
the joke)
3. water container
v. push, shove, bump
(goat butted her).

B104. buzz. n.
1. murmur, whisper,
hum 2. v. drone, whir.
(This is an
'onomatopoeic' word -
that is, it mimics the
sound it describes.)

C1. cabin. n. hut, shack, lodge, bungalow. A: mansion.

C2. cadge. v. beg, scrounge.

C3. calamity. n. disaster, mishap, catastrophe, ill fortune. A: benefit.

C4. callous. adj. unfeeling, cold, heartless. A: compassionate, sensitive.

C5. calm. adj. 1. smooth, still, unruffled (water) 2. peaceful, serene, composed v. soothe, quell, quiet. A: 1. rough, turbulent 2. agitated.

C6. cancel. v. call off, abandon, revoke, scrap. A: confirm, implement.

C7. capable. adj. able, competent, efficient, skillful. A: incapable, inept.

C8. caper. v. prance, dance, frisk, skip.

C9. caption. n. headline, title, heading.

C10. captivate. v. charm, fascinate, delight, bewitch. A: repulse.

C11. care. n. 1. caution, attention, carefulness (handle with care) 2. concern (care about) 3. anxiety, trouble, worry (not a care in the world) 4. charge, protection, keeping (in her care). A: 1. carelessness 2. unconcern 4. neglect.

C12. carefree. adj. untroubled, lighthearted, relaxed. A: careworn.

C13. careful. adj. 1. attentive, cautious 2. painstaking, meticulous. A: 1. reckless, lax 2. sloppy, slapdash.

C14. carnival. n. fair, festival, fete, gala.

C15. carry. v.
1. lift, bear, move (carry luggage) 2. transport, convey (carry passengers) 3. hold up, support (carry the weight of) 4. do, execute, perform (carry out my orders) 5. communicate, transmit, broadcast (papers carried the story).

C16. case. n.
1. instance, situation, incident (a case of mistaken identity)
2. patient, invalid (doctor attended the case)
3. box, crate, carton
4. inquiry, lawsuit, hearing (court case).

C17. casual. adj.
1. chance, unexpected, unplanned (meeting)
2. informal, easygoing, relaxed. A: 1. deliberate
2. formal.

C18. cause. v. bring about, give rise to, provoke n. 1. reason, source, motive 2. aim, object, purpose (good cause). A: v. prevent n. 1. result.

C19. cautious. adj. careful, wary, attentive.

C20. cease. v. stop, discontinue, finish, halt. A: commence, begin.

C21. celebrate. v.
1. commemorate, remember, observe
2. rejoice, revel.
A: ignore.

C22. cellar. n. basement, crypt, vault. A: attic. H: seller.

C23. centre. n. middle point, core, hub, heart. A: exterior, edge.

C24. cereal. n. grain, seed, meal, corn. H: serial.

C25. certain. adj.
1. sure, positive, convinced 2. definite, inevitable, unavoidable.
A: 1. uncertain 2. unlikely.

C26. chance. n.
1. accident, coincidence, fate, luck (happened by chance) 2. possibility, risk (a good chance) 3. turn, opportunity (your chance).
A: 1. intent 2. certainty.

C27. change. v.
1. alter, adjust, modify 2. exchange, replace, swap 3. become (change into) n. cash, coins.
A: 2. keep 3. remain.

C28. chaos. n. turmoil, confusion, disorder.
A: order.

C29. characteristic.
adj. typical, representative, distinctive n. quality, trait, feature.

C30. chase. v.
1. follow, pursue, trail 2. drive away, shoo, put to flight.

C31. cheap. adj.
1. inexpensive, cut-price, reasonable 2. shoddy, inferior, trashy.
A: 1. expensive 2. superior.
H: cheep (sound made by chicks).

C32. cheat. v. swindle, trick, defraud, break the rules.

C33. check. v.
1. inspect, examine, look at 2. stop, block, hold back n. 1. inspection, examination 2. restraint, limitation. H: cheque.

C34. cheer. v.
1. applaud, shout 2. comfort, gladden n. 1. yell, hurrah 2. hope, assurance 3. gaiety, pleasure. A: v. 1. boo 2. discourage n. 3. despair.

C35. chew. v. munch, bite, gnaw, crunch.

C36. chill. n. coolness, iciness v. freeze, refrigerate adj. 1. cool, aloof, icy (chill greeting) 2. cold, biting, raw (chill wind). A: n. warmth adj. 1. friendly 2. balmy.

C37. choice. n. 1. alternative, option, preference (his own choice) 2. selection, variety, assortment (the choice of rings) adj. superior, good quality, best (choice produce). A: 1. command, necessity adj. inferior.

C38. chop. v. hew, hack, cut, cleave, split.

C39. chore. n. small job, household task, errand.

C40. chuckle. v. giggle, titter, laugh quietly. A: guffaw.

C41. circle. n. 1. ring. hoop, circuit 2. group, company, clique (circle of friends) v. encircle, border, revolve, move around. A: square.

C42. circumference. n. periphery, perimeter, boundary, border.

C43. circumstance. n. occurrence, event, fact.

C44. cite. v. 1. refer to, quote, specify 2. commend, mention, honour. A:1. ignore 2. condemn. H: sight.

C45. civil. adj. 1. polite, respectful, well-mannered 2. communal, public, citizen's A: 1. rude, impolite 2. state, military.

C46. claim. v. 1. ask for, demand, request 2. assert, maintain, declare. A: 1. deny 2. disclaim.

C47. clammy. adj. cold and damp, moist, sticky. A: dry, cool.

C48. clamour. n. uproar, commotion, noise v. shout, cry out, yell. A: n. silence v. whisper.

C49. clarify. v. explain, make clear. A: obscure, confuse.

C50. clear. adj. 1. colourless, transparent, pure (water) 2. distinct, audible (clear sound) 3. plain, obvious, evident (clear meaning) 4. visible, focused (clear picture) 5. coherent, lucid, understandable (clear explanation) 6. unmuddled, alert, discerning (clear thinking) 7. open, free, unblocked (way was clear) 8. bright, cloudless (clear sky) v. 1. evaporate, fade (mist cleared) 2. leap over, vault, jump (clear the fence) 3. empty, evacuate (clear the area).

C51. clever. adj. smart, bright, intelligent. A: dull, stupid.

C52. climate. n. 1. weather 2. mood, atmosphere.

C53. cling. v. stick to, fuse, cleave, adhere. A: separate.

C54. clog. n. wooden shoe v. block, obstruct, choke. A: v. unblock.

C55. close. v. 1. shut, fasten, lock 2. bar, barricade, block 3. conclude, end 4. connect, join, link (close the wound) adj. 1. near, next to 2. affectionate, fond, intimate (close to her brother) 7. airless, stuffy, muggy (close in here) 8. mean, stingy (close with her money).

C

C56. coarse. adj.
1. rough, hairy, scratchy
2. crude, vulgar,
offensive. A: 1. smooth
2. refined. H: course.

C57. coincide. v.
1. meet, occur
simultaneously
2. agree, correspond.
A: 1. diverge 2. disagree.

C58. cold. adj.
1. chilly, wintry, freezing
2. callous, unemotional,
indifferent. A: 1. hot
2. passionate, caring.

C59. collide. v. crash
into, meet head on.
A: miss, avoid (collision).

C60. colour. n. hue,
shade, tint, tone, dye.

C61. colossal. adj.
huge, vast, immense.
A: minute, tiny.

C62. column. n.
1. pole, post, pillar
2. file, line, queue
3. vertical list.

C63. comfort. v.
reassure, console, soothe
n. 1. solace, consolation
2. ease, luxury,
relaxation.
A: v. torment
n.1. aggravation
2. hardship.

C64. commence. v.
begin, start, originate
A: end, close.

C65. commonplace.
adj. ordinary, everyday,
normal. A: rare.

C66. compassion. n.
sympathy, pity,
tenderness.
A: apathy, indifference.

C67. compel. v.
force, make, drive.
A: deter, hinder.

C68. compensate. v.
make up, repay,
recompense. A: worsen.

C69. competent. adj.
capable, efficient,
experienced.
A: incompetent, unfit.

C70. compile. v.
arrange, put together,
collect, edit. A: scatter.

C71. complacent. adj.
self-satisfied, smug.
A: insecure.

C72. complain. v.
grumble, object, criticise.
A: praise, compliment.

C73. complete. v.
achieve, finish, make
whole, carry out adj.
entire, whole, undivided.
A: v. start, fail.

C74. complex. adj.
complicated, intricate,
puzzling, involved.
A: simple.

C75. comprehend. v.
understand, grasp, make
out.

C76. comprise. v.
include, consist of,
contain.

C77. compulsory. adj.
required, unavoidable,
enforced.
A: optional, voluntary.

C78. conceal. v. hide,
cover up, disguise, keep
secret. A: display, reveal.

C79. conceited. adj.
arrogant, boastful, self-
important. A: humble,
modest (conceit).

C80. conceive. v.
create, originate, think
up, invent (conceivable).

C81. concept. n.
idea, theory, thought.

C82. concern. n.
1. company, firm
2. affair, matter, business
(that's my concern)
3. care, interest,
thoughtfulness.
A: 3. indifference.

C83. concise. adj.
brief, terse, condensed.
A: rambling.

C

C84. conclude. v.
1. end, finish, complete
2. deduce, judge, reason
3. decide, resolve, settle.

C85. confess. v.
admit, own up. A: deny.

C86. confident. adj.
certain, assured, positive.
A: unsure, apprehensive.

C87. confuse. v.
1. baffle, bewilder, mislead 2. muddle, mix up.
A: 1.enlighten 2.untangle.

C88. connect. v.
1. attach, fasten, join
2. link, relate
A: 1.unfasten 2.dissociate.

C89. conscious. adj.
1. awake, aware
2. deliberate, intentional.
A: unconscious, unaware.

C90. consent. v.
agree, allow, approve.
A: dissent, refuse, balk.

C91. consider. v. think about, contemplate, study.

C92. considerate. adj.
thoughtful, kind,
attentive, helpful.
A: inconsiderate, selfish.

C93. console. v.
comfort, soothe,
sympathise.
A: aggravate, hurt.

C94. constant. adj.
1. loyal, true, faithful
2. fixed, unchanging
3. ceaseless, unrelenting.
A: 1. disloyal 2. variable
3. occasional.

C95. construct. v.
build, assemble, make.
A: demolish.

C96. consume. v.
1. eat, devour (food)
2. use up, deplete, spend
(consume all your savings).
A: conserve, save.

C97. contempt. n.
scorn, disgust, dislike,
loathing. A: respect.

C98. content. adj.
satisfied, happy,
comfortable.
A: unsatisfied, restless.

C99. continual. adj.
ceaseless, constant,
endless. A: irregular.

C100. contract. n. agreement, deal, legal document v. shrink, compress, reduce. A: v. expand, stretch.

C101. contradict. v. deny, oppose, dispute. A: confirm.

C102. control. v.
1. manage, supervise
2. subdue, restrain, curb
n. command, rule.

C103. convenient. adj. handy, useful, available, suitable. A: inconvenient, awkward.

C104. cope. v. manage, handle, endure, withstand.

C105. core. n. centre, heart, kernel, nucleus.

C106. correct. adj. accurate, exact, faultless, right v. cure, put right, rectify. A: adj. wrong v. spoil.

C107. corridor. n. hall, passage, aisle.

C108. corrode. v. eat away, rust, erode.

C109. cost. n. price, charge, amount, expense, value.

C110. cosy. adj. snug, homely, comfortable, relaxing.

C111. courage. n. valour, bravery, daring. A: cowardice.

C112. course. n.
1. route, direction, way
2. series (course of lectures). H: coarse.

C113. cower. v. cringe, shrink, flinch, grovel. A: swagger, terrorise.

C114. crack. n.
1. break, fracture, split, fissure v. break down (crack under pressure)
2. shot, sound, report (crack of gun-fire).

C

C115. crafty. adj.
cunning, sly, shrewd,
deceitful. A: open, frank.

C116. cram. v.
squeeze, stuff,
overcrowd. A: empty.

C117. crave. v. yearn,
desire, long for.
A: loathe, refuse.

C118. crawl. v. creep,
clamber, squirm, wriggle.
A: walk.

C119. creative. adj.
imaginative, original,
artistic, inventive. (create;
creator).

C120. credible. adj.
believable, likely,
reasonable. A: incredible.

C121. crooked. adj.
twisted, awry, warped,
bent. A: straight.

C122. cross. n.
1. crucifix 2. burden,
misfortune, ordeal
3. crossbreed
v. 1. delete, cancel (cross
off) 2. go across, travel
over, intersect (cross
over) adj. 1. annoyed,
angry, bad-tempered
2. intersecting, lying
crosswise (cross timbers).

C123. cruel. adj.
brutal, sadistic, vicious,
ruthless.
A: merciful, kind.

C124. crumb. n.
speck, fragment, particle,
morsel.

C125. crumple. v.
crease, crush, wrinkle.

C126. crush. v.
1. squash, mash,
squeeze, press
2. subdue, defeat.

C127. crutch. n.
prop, support.

C128. cryptic. adj.
obscure, puzzling,
mysterious, hidden
(cryptic message).

C129. cue. n.
1. signal, sign
2. billiard cue. H: queue.

C130. culprit. n.
guilty person, offender,
wrongdoer.

C131. cultured. adj.
civilised, educated, well-
read, refined.
A: uneducated.

C132. cumbersome.
adj. awkward, heavy,
unmanageable.
A: compact.

C133. cunning. adj.
shrewd, crafty, sly,
devious.
A: artless, ingenuous.

C134. curb. n.
1. edge, rim, border
2. restraint, control,
limitation.

C135. cure. v. 1. heal
2. smoke, preserve (cure
hams) n. remedy,
treatment.

C136. curl. v.
coil, loop, curve, twist.

C137. curt. adj.
abrupt, blunt, rude, terse.
A: friendly, courteous.

C138. cut. v.
1. lacerate, slash, gash,
slice 2. mow, trim, clip
(cut lawn) 3. shorten,
condense, abbreviate (cut
the story down) 4. snub,
ignore (cut me dead)
5. cross, intersect, go
through (road cuts
through gorge).

C139. cynical. adj.
sneering, scornful,
skeptical.
A: optimistic, credulous.

D

D1. dainty. adj.
delicate, fine, exquisite.
A: coarse.

D2. damage. n.
harm, hurt, injury
v. harm, mar, spoil.
A: improve, mend.

D3. damn. v. condemn,
denounce, curse.
A: commend, praise.

D4. damp. adj. moist,
clammy, wet. A: dry.

D5. dance. v. leap,
cavort, gyrate, prance.

D6. danger. n.
1. risk, hazard, peril
2. possibility, chance
(danger of catching cold).
A: 1. security, safety
(dangerous).

D7. dangle. v. suspend,
hang, swing, sway.

D8. dare. v.
1. to challenge
2. risk, venture.

D9. dark. adj. 1. black,
deeply coloured (dark
hair) 2. shadowy, murky,
dingy (dark place)
3. overcast (sky)
4. dismal, dreary, joyless
(dark times) 5. angry,
sullen, sombre (dark
mood) 6. hidden,
obscure (dark meaning).
A: 1. light 2. lit, bright
3. clear 4. joyful
5. happy 6. open.

D10. dash. v.
1. rush, race, run
2. hurl, throw (dash the
cup against the wall)
3. trace, drop (dash of
milk).

D11. daunt. v.
discourage, frighten,
intimidate. A: encourage.

D12. dauntless. adj.
fearless, unafraid.

D13. dawn. n.
daybreak, sunrise.

D14. daze. v. stun,
confuse, bewilder, numb.

D15. dazzle. v. blind,
glare, overwhelm, overawe.

D16. deaden. v.
muffle, diminish,
weaken, stifle.

D17. dear. adj.
1. costly, expensive
2. precious, loved.
A: 1. cheap 2. hated.

D18. debris. n.
wreckage, remains,
fragments.

D19. debt. n.
obligation, amount,
arrears, bill.

D20. decay. v. rot,
decompose, disintegrate,
go bad.
A: flourish, grow.

D21. deceased. adj.
dead.

D22. deceit. n.
dishonesty, deception,
fraud. A: honesty,
openness (deceitful;
deceive).

D23. decent. adj.
good, proper, suitable,
honourable.
A: improper, indecent.

D24. declare. v.
announce, reveal,
proclaim, state.

D25. decline. v.
1. refuse, reject
2. decrease, lessen, flag
3. slope downward.
A: 1. accept, agree
2. increase, improve
3. rise.

D26. dedicate. v.
1. commit, devote, give
completely 2. inscribe (in
honour of someone).

D27. deed. n.
1. action, feat, adventure
2. legal document.

D28. deep. adj.
1. far down (hole)
2. thick (snow)
3. intense, earnest (feelings)
4. absorbed, engrossed
(thought) 5. serious,
intellectual (conversation)
6. low, base (note).
A: 3. shallow, superficial
4. distracted
5. lighthearted.

D

D29. defect. n.
fault, flaw, blemish,
imperfection.

D30. defiant. adj.
disobedient, obstinate,
rebellious.
A: submissive, obedient.

D31. definite. adj.
1. sure, certain, positive
2. exact, distinct, clear.
A: 1. uncertain
2. unclear.

D32. deformed. adj.
distorted, disfigured,
twisted, marred.

D33. dejected. adj.
discouraged, depressed,
crestfallen. A: elated.

D34. delay. v.
1. hinder, hold up
2. postpone, suspend
3. dawdle, hesitate.
A: 1. expedite 3. hasten.

D35. delete. v. cancel,
cross out, erase. A: add.

D36. deliberate. adj.
1. meant, intentional,
planned, calculated
(remark) 2. careful,
unhurried (pace).

D37. delicious. adj.
tasty, luscious, appetising.
A: unpleasant, distasteful.

D38. demand. v.
ask, order, insist, claim
n. need (a demand for
more staff).

D39. demolish. v.
destroy, wreck, tear
down, dismantle.
A: build, restore.

D40. deny. v.
contradict, refute,
disclaim. A: confirm.

D41. depart. v. go,
leave, exit, set out.
A: arrive, remain.

D42. depend. v.
rely, trust, count on.

D43. deposit. v. 1. put
down, place, leave, store
2. dregs, sediment.
A: withdraw.

D44. depress. v.
1. sadden, dishearten
2. lessen, weaken
3. lower, press down.

D45. deprive. v. deny, withhold, take away, confiscate. A: give.

D46. deputy. n. assistant, replacement, stand-in.

D47. derelict. adj. abandoned, deserted, forsaken, dilapidated.

D48. deride. v. ridicule, mock, jeer.

D49. descend. v.
1. drop, go down
2. dip, slope 3. swoop, invade (descend upon).
A: ascend.

D50. describe. v. explain, depict, tell, relate, draw (describe a circle).

D51. desert. v. forsake, abandon
n. wasteland, wilderness.

D52. desire. v. crave, want, wish for, long for.
A: spurn, dislike.

D53. desolate. adj.
1. bleak, barren, deserted (place)
2. forlorn, sad, melancholy, (person)
A: 1. inhabited
2. cheerful.

D54. despair. n. hopelessness, depression, gloom
A: hopefulness.

D55. destiny. n. fate, fortune, lot, future.

D56. destitute. adj. penniless, poor, poverty-stricken. A: rich.

D57. destroy. v. ruin, demolish, annihilate, devastate.
A: save, preserve.

D58. detached. adj.
1. separate
2. disinterested, impartial, neutral, uninvolved.
A: 1. attached
2. biased, involved.

D

D59. detail. n.
feature, item, point, fact.

D60. detain. v. delay,
hold, hinder, slow up.

D61. detect. v.
discover, notice, observe,
spot.

D62. determined. adj.
resolved, intent, firm,
steadfast.
A: doubtful: hesitant.

D63. detest. v. loathe,
hate, dislike. A: like, love.

D64. detour. v.
go around, bypass.

D65. device. n.
1. gadget, tool,
instrument
2. trick, scheme, ruse.

D66. devour. v.
eat greedily, gobble, bolt,
gulp. A: refuse.

D67. dialect. n.
accent, brogue, idiom.

D68. dialogue. n.
conversation, discussion,
talk.

D69. die. v. perish,
expire, pass away.
A: live, survive.

D70. differ. v.
1. disagree (differ with)
2. contrast, stand apart,
be unlike (differ from).
A: 1. agree
2. mimic, copy.

D71. difficult. adj.
hard, advanced,
laborious, complicated.
A: easy, simple.

D72. dig. v. scoop,
gouge, excavate.

D73. dignified. adj.
sedate, noble, stately,
formal.
A: undignified, vulgar.

D74. dim. adj.
indistinct, faint, hazy,
gloomy. A: bright, clear.

D75. din. n. clamour,
uproar, racket, hubbub.
A: quiet, calm.

D76. dip. v.
1. immerse briefly, sub-merge 2. ladle, scoop
3. sink, decline, slope
4. try, study slightly, skim (dip into a book)
n. dent, depression, hollow.

D77. dirty. adj.
1. filthy, grimy, mucky, dusty 2. coarse, crude, offensive (language)
3. unpleasant, difficult, disagreeable (jobs).

D78. disappoint. v. let down, sadden, disillusion. A: gratify, satisfy.

D79. disaster. n. catastrophe, calamity, misfortune, tragedy. A: blessing.

D80. discard. v. throw away, dispose of. A: retain, keep.

D81. discharge. v.
1. shoot, fire (a gun)
2. dismiss, sack
3. release, acquit, free.

D82. discomfort. n.
1. distress, pain, ache
2. uneasiness, embarrassment, worry. A: comfort, ease.

D83. discreet. adj. careful, tactful, prudent, guarded. A: rash.

D84. disdain. v. despise, dislike, look down on, snub. A: admire.

D85. disgrace. n. shame, dishonour, humiliation.

D86. disgust. n. distaste, revulsion, repulsion. A: delight.

D87. dishevelled. adj. unkempt, rumpled, untidy, bedraggled. A: neat, groomed.

D88. dismal. adj. bleak, cheerless, dreary, gloomy. A: bright, cheerful.

D

D89. dismay. v.
alarm, appal, distress
n. anxiety, fright,
apprehension.
A: v. reassure n. relief.

D90. display. v.
exhibit, show,
demonstrate.

D91. dispute. v. argue,
debate, quarrel.
A: agree.

D92. disreputable.
adj. shady,
dishonourable,
disgraceful. A: reputable.

D93. disrupt. v.
interrupt, interfere with,
break-up, upset.

D94. dissolve. v.
1. melt, liquefy 2. end,
disband.

D95. dissuade. v.
advise against,
discourage.

D96. distend. v. swell,
bloat, expand.

D97. distinct. adj.
1. different, dissimilar
2. clear, plain, defined.
A: 1. similar 2. obscure.

D98. distort. v. warp,
twist, misrepresent (truth).

D99. distract. v.
divert, confuse, bewilder,
amuse.

D100. distribute. v.
dispense, give out, allot,
circulate, deliver.

D101. disturb. v.
1. interrupt, bother
2. unsettle, alarm, upset.
A: establish.

D102. diverge. v.
branch, separate, divide.
A: converge.

D103. dizzy. adj.
giddy, confused,
unsteady.

D104. docile. adj.
gentle, meek, obedient,
tame. A: unruly, wild.

D105. dock. n.
berth, wharf, harbour,
port
v. cut off, cut short.

D106. dodge. v. duck,
swerve, avoid, evade.

D107. domain. n.
territory, property,
realm, sphere.

D108. dominate. v.
control, rule, direct,
govern.

D109. donate. v.
give, grant, supply.

D110. doom. n.
destiny, fate.

D111. dormant. v.
asleep, inactive, resting,
hibernating. A: active.

D112. dose. n.
portion, amount.

D113. doubt. n.
misgiving, hesitation,
uncertainty.
A: confidence, belief.

D114. downtrodden.
adj. oppressed,
exploited, tyrannised.

D115. doze. v.
snooze, nap.

D116. drab. adj.
dull, dingy, dreary.

D117. drag. v.
pull, haul, draw, lug.

D118. drastic. adj.
extreme, intense, severe.
A: mild.

D119. draw. v.
1. sketch 2. pull, tow,
haul 3. attract, lure,
entice (draw a crowd)
4. take out, extract (draw
out) 5. deduce, infer
(draw a conclusion)
n. raffle, lottery (prize
draw).

D

D120. dread. n. fear, horror, apprehension. A: courage, fearlessness.

D121. dribble. v. drip, trickle, seep, ooze.

D122. drift. v. 1. float, glide 2. wander, amble, meander n. 1. pile, heap (snow drift) 2. meaning, sense, direction (drift of speech).

D123. drive. v.
1. pilot, steer, operate
2. force, press, compel
3. push, surge, advance
n. 1. ride, outing
2. ambition, energy, motivation.

D124. drivel. n. nonsense, twaddle, gibberish.

D125. droop. v. sag, flop, wilt. A: revive, perk up.

D126. drop. n.
1. droplet, tear, globule
2. dash, trace, spot
3. slope, plunge, abyss
v. 1. fall, plummet, dive
2. abandon, leave, give up (drop the subject).

D127. drowsy. adj. sleepy, dozy, listless, tired. A: alert.

D128. drudgery. n. toil, labour, grind.

D129. dry. adj.
1. rainless, arid, parched
2. thirsty 3. dull, boring (dry lecture) 4. witty, droll (dry humour)
v. 1. wipe, blot
2. shrivel, dehydrate, wilt.

D130. dual. adj. twofold, double, coupled. H: duel.

D131. dud. adj. useless, worthless.

D132. due. adj.
1. owing, unpaid
2. suitable, fitting, appropriate (due consideration)
3. scheduled, expected (train due at).

D133. duel. n. fight, shoot-out, contest.
H: dual.

D134. dull. adj.
1. blunt 2. dense, slow, stupid 3. boring, uninteresting 4. muffled, indistinct (sound) 5. drab, muted, sombre (colour) 6. sunless, overcast (sky).

D135. dumb. adj.
mute, silent, speechless.

D136. duplicate. n.
copy, replica, imitation.
A: original.

D137. durable. adj.
lasting, hard-wearing, sturdy. A: flimsy.

D138. dusk. n.
twilight, sunset, evening, nightfall.

D139. duty. n.
1. responsibility, loyalty
2. task, chore, assignment 3. tax, tariff.

D140. dwell. v. reside, inhabit, live, abide.
A: roam.

D141. dwindle. v.
shrink, lessen, diminish, wane. A: increase, grow.

D142. dye. n.
colour, tint, stain, shade.

D143. dynamic. adj.
vigorous, energetic, powerful, active.
A: weak, lethargic.

E

E1. eager. adj. keen, excited, enthusiastic, impatient.
A: indifferent, opposed.

E2. early. adv. 1. first, initial (early appointment) 2. before time, prematurely (early arrival) 3. ancient, historic (early man). A: 1. later 2. late 3. modern.

E3. earn. v. 1. deserve, merit 2. make, receive, get. A: 1. waste, spend 2. forfeit.

E4. earnest. adj. 1. serious, solemn 2. sincere, whole hearted, determined. A: 1. frivolous 2. insincere.

E5. ease. n. 1. comfort, relaxation, luxury 2. relief, freedom from pain 3. effortlessness 4. naturalness, unaffectedness. v. 1. relieve, assuage, soothe 2. move carefully, manoeuvre.

A: 1. poverty 2. discomfort 3. difficulty 4. formality, affectedness. v. worsen, irritate.

E6. eat. v. dine, consume, chew, devour. A: fast, starve.

E7. ebb. v. recede, flow, go back, retreat.

E8. eccentric. adj. odd, strange, abnormal, weird, uncommon. A: normal.

E9. echo. v. repeat, resound, reverberate, imitate.

E10. edge. n. border, boundary, brink, fringe, rim, side. A: centre.

E11. edit. v. correct, check, rewrite, amend.

E12. educate. v. teach, instruct, enlighten, train, inform.

E13. eerie. adj. creepy, frightening, weird, spooky, ghostly. A: comforting.

E14. effect. n. 1. consequence, outcome, result 2. impression, impact 3. fact, truth, intent (in effect) 4. personal property, possessions.

E15. efficient. adj. effective, capable, productive, businesslike. A: inefficient, wasteful.

E16. effort. n. 1. exertion, strain, toil, work 2. try, attempt.

E17. eject. v. 1. throw out, emit 2. drive out, banish, expel. A: 1. retain 2. admit.

E18. elaborate. adj. 1. complex, complicated, involved 2. fancy, showy, ornate. v. expand, add details, embellish.

A: 1. simple 2. plain 3. abbreviate.

E19. elastic. adj. flexible, springy, stretchable.

E20. elated. adj. delighted, jubilant, ecstatic, overjoyed. A: despondent, discouraged.

E21. elect. v. choose, pick, select by vote. A: reject, defeat.

E22. elegant. adj. 1. grand, classic, tasteful (place) 2. refined, dignified, polished (person). A: 1. ugly, tawdry 2. coarse, ungraceful.

E23. element. n. 1. basic part, ingredient, component 2. chemical substance 3. weather 4. environment, natural surroundings (out of his element).

E

E24. elevate. v.
1. raise, lift, move up
2. promote.
A: 1. lower 2. demote.

E25. eligible. adj.
suitable, qualified,
acceptable.
A: unsuitable.

E26. eliminate. v. get
rid of, eradicate, abolish,
stamp out. A: establish.

E27. elude. v. avoid,
dodge, evade, escape.
A: confront.

E28. elusive. adj. hard
to catch, wily, evasive.

E29. emblem. n.
badge, crest, insignia,
seal.

E30. embrace. v.
1. hug, clasp, cuddle
2. accept, adopt, include.

E31. emerge. v.
develop, appear, come
out, evolve, show.
A: recede, fade away.

E32. emigrate. v.
move, leave, depart, quit.
A: immigrate.

E33. emit. v. discharge,
send out, expel, issue.
A: retain, inject.

E34. emotion. n.
passion, feeling,
sentiment, fervour.
A: indifference.

E35. emphasise. v.
stress, feature,
accentuate, underline.
A: play down.

E36. employ. v.
1. use 2. give work to,
hire 3. keep busy,
occupy, involve.
A: 1. waste, dismiss.

E37. empty. adj.
1. vacant, deserted,
unoccupied (house)
2. bare, unfurnished
(room) 3. hollow, void
(space) 4. blank, clean,
unused (page)
5. purposeless, futile (life)
A: 1. inhabited
2. furnished 3. full,
crammed 4. marked,
filled 5. meaningful,
interesting.

E38. enable. v.
make able, empower,
allow, assist.
A: prevent, hinder.

E39. encounter. v.
meet, run into, confront
n. battle, fight,
confrontation.
A: 1. elude, miss
2. retreat.

E40. encourage. v.
1. inspire, cheer up,
reassure, hearten
2. promote, help, foster
(advertising encourages
sales) 3. invite, prompt,
urge (encourage people
to come).
A: 1. discourage,
dishearten 2. hinder,
retard 3. dissuade.

E41. endeavour. v.
try, attempt, strive.
A: neglect.

E42. endure. v.
1. bear, suffer,
withstand, sustain 2. last,
continue, prevail
A: 1. avoid, escape
2. perish, fail.

E43. enemy. n.
foe, adversary, rival,
opponent. A: friend.

E44. energy. n.
power, force, vitality,
vigour.
A: inertia, lassitude.

E45. enjoy. v.
appreciate, delight in,
take pleasure in, have
the benefit of.
A: detest, hate.

E46. enough. adj.
ample, sufficient,
adequate. A: insufficient.

E47. enrol. v.
sign up, register, join.

E48. enterprising. adj.
resourceful, ambitious,
hard-working,
adventurous.
A: lazy, timid.

E49. enthusiasm. n.
1. keenness, eagerness,
excitement
2. craze, interest, hobby.
A: 1. apathy, coolness.

E50. entire. adj.
complete, total, whole,
intact. A: partial, broken.

E51. envious. adj.
jealous, covetous,
resentful, grudging.

E

E52. episode. n.
instalment, section, passage.

E53. equal. adj. even, identical, matched, the same, balanced.
A: unequal, uneven.

E54. equip. v. provide, supply, outfit. A: divest.

E55. era. n.
period, age, time.

E56. err. v.
make a mistake, slip up, miscalculate, do wrong.

E57. erratic. adj.
inconsistent, changeable, unpredictable, variable.
A: constant.

E58. escort. v.
accompany, guide, guard, date.

E59. essential. adj.
1. basic, fundamental, principal 2. necessary, vital. A: dispensable, unimportant.

E60. estate. n.
1. property, land
2. possessions, wealth, inheritance.

E61. eternal. adj.
endless, timeless, infinite.
A: transitory, perishable.

E62. evade. v.
dodge, elude, escape.

E63. even. adj. 1. level, flat, smooth 2. constant, regular (even speed)
3. calm, placid, serene (even temper).

E64. event. n.
1. happening, incident, occurrence 2. contest, competition, match.

E65. evict. v.
throw out, dislodge, expel, oust.

E66. evolve. v.
develop, grow, emerge.

E67. exact. adj.
precise, accurate, specific, correct.
A: approximate (exactly).

E68. exaggerate. v.
overstate, magnify,
enlarge on, embroider.
A: understate.

E69. examine. v.
inspect, study, scrutinise,
check, investigate.
A: ignore, accept.

E70. exceed. v. outdo,
go beyond, surpass, go
over. A: stay within.

E71. excellent. adj.
outstanding, brilliant,
superior, exceptional.
A: imperfect, poor.

E72. excite. v. agitate,
arouse, provoke,
stimulate, thrill.
A: bore, lull.

E73. exclude. v. bar,
ban, shut out, omit,
prohibit. A: include.

E74. excuse. v.
forgive, pardon, make
allowance for
n. explanation, defence,
justification. A: v. blame,
punish n. accusation.

E75. exert. v. put
forth, attempt, exercise,
apply (exert your energy).

E76. exhausted. adj.
worn out, tired, fatigued,
wearied. A: refreshed.

E77. exist. v.
be, endure, live, survive,
occur. A: die, disappear.

E78. exotic. adj.
1. foreign, strange
2. striking, colourful,
vivid, rich.
A: 1. native 2. dull.

E79. expand. v.
enlarge, amplify, widen,
extend, spread, develop.
A: contract.

E80. expect. v.
rely upon, hope for,
anticipate, foresee.
A: despair of.

E81. expensive. adj.
costly, dear, overpriced,
extravagant. A: cheap.

E

E82. experience. n.
1. event, incident
2. knowledge, practice
v. know, undergo, live
through, suffer.
A: 2. inexperience,
theory v. miss.

E83. expert. n.
authority, specialist,
professional adj. skilled,
experienced, talented.
A: n. amateur
adj. incompetent.

E84. exploit. n.
feat, act, deed
v. use, take advantage
of. A: n. failure
v. pass up, ignore.

E85. explore. v.
1. scout, travel and
observe, traverse
2. investigate, examine,
look into.

E86. explosion. n.
blast, bang, eruption,
detonation.

E87. export. v.
sell abroad, dispatch.
A: import.

E88. expose. v.
1. uncover, bare, display,
leave unprotected
2. disclose, divulge,
reveal. A: 1. hide,
protect 2. conceal.

E89. exquisite. adj.
beautiful, delicate, dainty,
elegant. A: clumsy, ugly.

E90. extent. n.
amount, area,
dimension, range,
measurement (extensive).

E91. exterior. n.
outside, surface, shell,
skin.
A: interior (external).

E92. extinct. adj. dead,
gone, defunct, vanished.
A: extant, surviving.

E93. extinguish. v.
1. put out, quench,
douse 2. wipe out,
destroy, eliminate.
A: 1. ignite 2. foster,
promote.

E94. extract. v.
1. pull out 2. get, obtain, derive 3. choose, select, abstract, quote.
A: 1. implant, insert.

E95. extraordinary.
adj. remarkable, rare, phenomenal, amazing.
A: usual, average.

E96. extreme. adj.
1. intense, severe, excessive 2. farthest, most distant
3. advanced, radical, outrageous (extreme views).
A: 1. moderate, average
2. nearest
3. conservative.

E97. exuberant. adj.
enthusiastic, vigorous, energetic, excited.
A: dispirited.

F1. fable. n. fairy tale, myth, legend.

F2. fact. n.
data, information, truth, evidence, reality.

F3. fade. v.
1. discolour, bleach, pale
2. wane, diminish, dwindle, decline.
A: 1. brighten 2. flourish.

F4. fail. v. 1. miss, not succeed 2. disappoint, let down, neglect (fail to call)
3. weaken, decline, deteriorate (failing health).
A: 1. succeed 2. support
3. improve, wax.

F5. fake. adj. false, bogus, forged
v. pretend, simulate, hoax, forge.
A: adj. real, authentic.

F6. falter. v. hesitate, waver, halt, stumble.
A: proceed.

F7. familiar. adj.
1. well-known, common, everyday, regular
2. friendly, amicable, intimate (familiar face).
A: 1. new, rare
2. unknown.

F

F8. famished. adj. starving, hungry, ravenous. A: full, replete.

F9. far. adv. adj. remote, distant, yonder. A: near, close.

F10. fare. n. charge, cost, price, ticket. H: fair.

F11. fascinate. v. charm, entrance, captivate, bewitch (fascinating).

F12. fatal. adj. terminal, lethal, deadly, destructive. A: harmless.

F13. fate. n. destiny, karma, fortune, providence.

F14. fault. n. 1. defect, imperfection, short-coming, flaw 2. blame, guilt. A: 1. virtue, strength 2. credit, praise.

F15. favour. n.
1. kindness, good turn
2. approval, esteem
3. support, sanction, like (favour the idea).

F16. fear. n. terror, alarm, dread, panic. A: confidence, fearlessness.

F17. feast. n. banquet, repast, large dinner. A: famine, fast.

F18. feat. n. deed, act, exploit, achievement. H: feet.

F19. feature. n.
1. highlight, main item (feature film) 2. aspect, characteristic, detail
3. part of the face.

F20. fee. n. charge, price, payment, hire.

F21. feel. v. 1. touch, handle 2. experience, sense, suffer (feel the cold) 3. fumble, grope (feel for the light) 4. think, believe, be convinced (feel about) 5. sympathise, have compassion (feel for).

F22. fend. v. ward off, avert, parry, repel.

F23. ferocious. adj. savage, vicious, ravening, enraged. A: tame, mild.

F24. festive. adj. merry, joyful, gay, light-hearted. A: gloomy, drab.

F25. feud. n. quarrel, hostility, vendetta, conflict.

F26. fiasco. n. failure, disaster, flop. A: success, triumph.

F27. fickle. adj. changeable, inconsistent, flighty, unreliable. A: constant.

F28. fidget. v. wriggle, twitch, fuss, squirm (fidgety).

F29. fierce. adj. savage, menacing, ferocious. A: docile, harmless.

F30. fight. n. 1. battle, contest, skirmish, struggle 2. quarrel, feud, row 3. spirit, pluck, grit.

F31. file. v.
1. sort, classify, group
2. march, parade
3. smooth, sand, grind n. column, line, queue.

F32. fill. v. 1. load, pack, cram 2. occupy (fill the seats) 3. supply, provide (fill the order) A: 1,2. empty (full)

F33. final. adj. last, deciding, ultimate, closing, conclusive A: first, opening.

F34. finish. v.
1. complete, conclude, stop, terminate
2. perfect, refine (finish the job) 3. kill, destroy, exterminate (finish off). A: begin.

F35. finite. adj. limited, measurable, bounded. A: eternal, infinite.

F

F36. fire. v. 1. burn, ignite, kindle 2. shoot, discharge, detonate 3. dismiss, sack 4. arouse, excite, stir (fire the imagination). A: 1. douse 3. hire 4. calm.

F37. firm. adj. 1. stiff, hard, rigid (firm floor) 2. resolute, dogged, adamant (firm resolve) 3. settled, fixed, unchangeable (firm arrangement) 4. secure, steady, immovable (firm construction) n. business, company. A: 1. soft 2. wavering, undecided 3. flexible 4. loose, unstable.

F38. fit. adj. 1. suitable, right, appropriate 2. healthy, capable, prepared (fit for action) v. assemble, build, construct n. attack, seizure, outbreak. A: 1. unsuitable 2. unfit, inadequate.

F39. fix. v. 1. fasten, attach (fix to) 2. settle, decide, agree (fix at) 3. mend, repair, adjust (fix the broken bike) n. dilemma, difficulty, awkward situation (in a fix).

F40. fixed. adj. immovable, firm, constant, steady. A: moving.

F41. flair. n. 1. talent, aptitude, knack 2. style, dash, panache. H: flare.

F42. flatter. v. praise, compliment (flattery).

F43. flaw. n. blemish, fault, defect, imperfection, mistake.

F44. flee. v. escape, run away, abscond. H: flea.

F45. flexible. adj. bendable, pliable, springy, supple. A: rigid.

F46. flicker. v. flutter, glimmer, waver, shimmer.

F47. flimsy. adj. delicate, fragile, sheer, diaphanous. A: stout, solid.

F48. flinch. v. wince, shrink, recoil, draw back.

F49. fling. v. hurl, toss, sling, throw.

F50. flippant. adj. disrespectful, frivolous, brash, pert. A: respectful.

F51. float. v. drift, hover, bob, waft. A: sink.

F52. flood. n. torrent, deluge, cascade v. submerge, drown, drench. A: n. drought.

F53. floor. n. 1. base, bottom surface, ground 2. level, store v. defeat, overcome, upset, overthrow.

F54. flop. v. 1. topple, collapse, droop, fall 2. fail, close down (the show flopped).

F55. flounce. v. stomp, storm, fling, bounce n. frill, ruffle.

F56. flourish. v. 1. prosper, thrive, grow 2. brandish, swing, shake.

F57. fluctuate. v. rise and fall, change often, *ebb and flow.* A: hold fast.

F58. fluid. n. liquid, solution adj. 1. watery, runny 2. flexible, adaptable.

F59. flush. v. 1. blush, redden, colour 2. wash out, rinse out.

F60. flux. n. 1. flow, current, tide 2. continuous change, alteration, transition (a state of flux).

F61. foe. n. enemy, attacker, adversary, rival. A: friend.

F62. fog. n. 1. haze, mist, smog 2. daze, stupor, bewilderment (brain in a fog).

F63. foil. v. hinder, block, prevent, obstruct. A: abet, further.

F64. follow. v. 1. come next, ensue, replace 2. pursue, chase, trail 3. obey, heed (follow the instructions) 4. copy, emulate (follow his example).

F

F65. fond. adj. affectionate, tender, loving, partial, doting.

F66. fool. n. 1. idiot, simpleton, half-wit, moron 2. clown, jester v. deceive, trick, mislead.

F67. forbid. v. ban, bar, refuse, prohibit, veto A: allow, permit.

F68. force. n. 1. energy, might, power 2. team, gang, crew v. compel, oblige, constrain, make. A: 1. weakness, ineffectiveness v. request.

F69. forecast. v. predict, project, calculate, foretell, expect.

F70. foreign. adj. not native, unfamiliar, alien, imported, strange. A: native.

F71. foremost. adj. main, chief, principal.

F72. forestall. v. prevent, ward off.

F73. forgery. n. fake, copy, imitation, replica.

F74. forget. v. overlook, neglect, omit, disregard. A: remember.

F75. forgive. n. pardon, excuse, overlook, absolve. A: blame, condemn.

F76. fortitude. n. endurance, courage, pluck, bravery.

F77. fortune. n. 1. destiny, luck, fate 2. wealth, riches, treasure.

F78. foul. adj. 1. disgusting, revolting, filthy 2. rough, stormy, windy (weather) 3. offensive, crude, vulgar (language) 4. wicked, heinous, contemptible (crime) 5. polluted, impure (air). A: 1. clean, spotless 2. mild 3. exemplary, modest 5. clear.

F79. fragile. adj. brittle, delicate, breakable. A: tough.

F80. frank. adj. direct, outspoken, candid, honest.

F81. free. adj.
1. released, liberated.
2. able, allowed
3. generous, lavish (free with his money)
4. complimentary, gratis, for nothing (free gift)
5. uninhibited, informal, lax (free and easy). A: 1. enslaved 2. restrained 3. mean 5. reserved.

F82. fresh. adj. new, recent, original, unused. A: stale, old, unoriginal.

F83. frivolous. adj. trivial, silly, flippant, unserious. A: important, sensible.

F84. frown. v. scowl, glower, glare. A: smile.

F85. fulfil. v. accomplish, do, complete, achieve. A: neglect, fail.

F86. function. n.
1. purpose, task, use, objective 2. event, reception, party v. act, behave, perform.

F87. fundamental. adj. basic, essential, crucial, underlying. A: advanced.

F88. furious. adj. angry, irate, enraged, mad. A: calm, pleased.

F89. furnish. v. equip, provide, supply.

F90. furrow. n. groove, rut, channel, depression.

F91. furtive. adj. stealthy, sly, secretive. A: forthright.

F92. futile. adj. useless, vain, ineffective, unsuccessful. A: effective, fruitful.

F93. fuzzy. adj.
1. blurred, indistinct, hazy 2. woolly, frizzy, fluffy.

G

G1. gadget. n.
device, tool, instrument, machine.

G2. gain. v. 1. get, obtain, acquire 2. reach, arrive at, attain (gain your objective). A: lose.

G3. gamble. v.
bet, wager, risk, chance. H: gambol.

G4. gap. n.
1. opening, break, hole
2. interval, lull, pause.

G5. gape. v.
stare open-mouthed, gawk, stare.

G6. garbage. n.
rubbish, trash, litter, junk. A: treasure.

G7. garnish. v.
decorate, trim, embellish.

G8. gash. n.
slash, cut, slit, wound.

G9. gasp. v.
pant, puff, wheeze.

G10. gather. v.
1. collect, amass
2. assemble, group, convene 3. deduce, assume, understand (gather from your remarks). A: disperse.

G11. gaudy. adj. lurid, tasteless, flashy, loud. A: tasteful, refined.

G12. gauge. v.
estimate, judge, guess, calculate.

G13. gaunt. adj.
emaciated, skinny, bony, starved. A: plump, sleek.

G14. gay. adj. light-hearted, merry, gleeful. A: grave.

G15. gaze. v.
stare, study, scrutinise. A: glance.

G16. generate. v.
1. create, breed
2. cause, produce, bring about.

G17. genuine. adj.
1. authentic, actual, real
2. sincere, honest, open.
A: 1. fake, false
2. insincere.

G18. germ. n.
1. microbe, virus, bacteria
2. bud, sprout, seed.

G19. gesture. n.
sign, motion,
e.g. shrug, nod, wave.

G20. get. v. 1. obtain, acquire, gain 2. bring, fetch, retrieve 3. catch, develop, contract (get a cold) 3. arrive, reach (get to) 4. understand, grasp, perceive (get the point) 5. persuade, coax, influence (get him to do it).

G21. ghastly. adj.
hideous, grisly, horrifying, gruesome.

G22. giddy. adj. dizzy, faint, reeling, unsteady.

G23. gift. n.
1. present, donation, offering 2. talent, aptitude, flair. A: 1. penalty.

G24. gingerly. adv.
cautiously, warily, timidly.
A: boldly, carelessly.

G25. girth. n.
circumference, dimensions, length around.

G26. give. v.
1. present, donate, award 2. hand over, pass to 3. tell, reveal (give me the facts) 4. allow, enable, grant (give him the chance) 5. collapse, break (give under the weight). A: 1. receive 2. take 3. conceal 4. withhold.

G27. glad. adj. pleased, delighted, happy.
A: sad, sorry.

G28. glance. v. look quickly, peep, peek, scan A: inspect, study.

G29. glare. n.
1. scowl, glower, frown
2. gleam, flare, glow.

G

G30. glaze. n.
gloss, varnish, lustre,
sugarcoat.

G31. glib. adj. flippant,
slick, smooth, suave.
A: sincere, deliberate.

G32. glide. v.
skim, slide, flow, drift.

G33. glimpse. v.
notice, see, catch sight
of, espy.
A: survey, observe.

G34. glitter. v. sparkle,
glisten, gleam, glint.

G35. gloat. v. brag,
boast, crow over, relish
maliciously.
A: regret, deplore.

G36. gloomy. adj.
1. dismal, dark, dingy,
shadowy (place) 2. glum,
downcast, miserable,
forlorn (person).
A: 1. bright, sunny
2. happy, blithe.

G37. glorious. adj.
1. beautiful, splendid,
magnificent, radiant
2. celebrated,
distinguished, famous
(glorious victory).
A: 1. horrible 2. trivial.

G38. glow. v.
1. burn, shine, radiate
2. blush, redden, tingle.

G39. glut. n.
oversupply, surplus,
excess.
A: shortage, dearth.

G40. gnarled. adj.
knotted, lumpy, twisted,
distorted.

G41. gnaw. v. chew,
bite, chomp.

G42. go. v. 1. set off,
begin, leave, proceed
2. extend, reach, stretch
to (belt goes round)
3. function, perform,
operate (car won't go)
4. elapse, pass (time
goes by) 5. fit, belong
(where does this go?)

6. become (go mad)
7. continue, keep on, persevere (go on)
8. accompany, escort (go with) 9. endure, experience, survive (go through).

G43. goods. n. possessions, property, cargo, merchandise.

G44. gorgeous. adj. stunning, ravishing, resplendent, lovely. A: ugly, drab, cheap, plain.

G45. gory. adj. 1. bloody, bloodstained 2. bloodcurdling, scary.

G46. gossip. n. 1. rumour, scandal, backbiting, hearsay 2. busybody, snoop, meddler, talebearer.

G47. govern. n. manage, control, direct, administer.

G48. grab. v. snatch, seize, clutch, pluck, grasp. A: release.

G49. grace. n. 1. elegance, lissomeness, fluidity 2. mercy, pardon, lenience, God's favour 3. extra time, reprieve, exemption (30 days' grace).

G50. gradual. adj. steady, even, paced, regular. A: sudden.

G51. grand. adj. impressive, great, majestic, stately. A: paltry, inferior.

G52. grate. v. 1. shred 2. scrape, rasp, grind 3. irritate, jar, annoy. n. fireplace, hearth. A: 2. slide, glide 3. soothe. H: great.

G53. gratitude. n. gratefulness, thankfulness, appreciation. A: ingratitude.

G54. grave. adj. 1. solemn, earnest, thoughtful (person) 2. serious, urgent, critical (matter) n. burial-place, tomb. A: 1. carefree, gay 2. insignificant.

G

G55. great. adj.
1. vast, huge, enormous
2. outstanding, remarkable, superior (great achievement)
3. distinguished, eminent, famous, gifted (person) 4. close, valued, loved (friend)
5. enjoyable, good, pleasant (great time).
A: 1. tiny, insignificant
2. average, unremark-able 3. mediocre.
H: grate.

G56. greet. v.
welcome, meet, receive.
A: ignore, bid farewell.

G57. grief. n. sorrow, misery, heartbreak, desolation.
A: solace, joy.

G58. grim. adj.
1. gloomy, severe, morose, sulky 2. sinister, grisly, menacing, ominous. A: cheerful, congenial, pleasant.

G59. grind. v.
1. pulverise, crush, mill
2. sharpen, file, whet
n. drudgery, chore, hard work.

G60. groan. v. moan, grumble, grunt, murmur.

G61. grope. v. fumble, feel about, scrabble.

G62. gross. adj.
1. total, whole, entire (gross profit) 2. flagrant, utter, obvious, outrageous (gross negligence) 3. obese, huge, monstrous.

G63. grouse. v. grumble, complain.

G64. grove. n.
copse, coppice, thicket, woodland.

G65. grow. v.
1. cultivate, sow, plant
2. emerge, germinate, sprout 3. flourish, thrive, ripen 4. become taller, expand, increase, spread
5. mature, develop. A: 4. shrink, diminish, wane.

G66. grudge. n. resentment, ill will, spite, envy. A: goodwill, friendliness.

G67. gruelling. adj. exhausting, tiring, laborious. A: easy.

G68. guess. v. assume, estimate, suspect, deduce, suppose. A: know.

G69. guide. n. 1. pilot, leader, escort 2. adviser, teacher, example 3. signpost, beacon, marker.

G70. gulf. n. 1. large bay 2. chasm, separation, rift, gap, abyss.

G71. gulp. v. swig, swallow, bolt, guzzle. A: sip, nibble.

G72. gush. v. 1. spurt, rush, pour, flow 2. be effusive, prattle, fuss.

G73. gust. n. wind, squall, flurry, puff.

G74. guttural. adj. throaty, husky, deep, hoarse (voice).

G75. gyrate. v. rotate, spin, revolve, twirl.

H1. habit. n. 1. religious dress. 2. custom, practice, routine.

H2. hack. v. chop, hew, slash, cut.

H3. hall. n. passage, corridor, lobby.

H4. halt. v. stop, draw up, come to a standstill, cease. A: continue.

H5. hamper. v. hinder, impede, obstruct, hold up. A: help.

H6. handy. adj. 1. convenient, close at hand 2. skillful, capable (handyman) A: 1. inaccessible 2. useless.

H

H7. hang. v.
1. suspend, dangle
2. droop, sag 3. drift, hover 4. loiter, linger (hang about) 5. hesitate (hang back) 6. execute. (Note past tenses: 'hung' for curtains, picture, etc.; 'hanged' for a person).

H8. happen. v.
1. occur, take place
2. chance, turn out (happened to meet).

H9. happy. adj.
glad, content, delighted, merry.
A: sad, melancholy.

H10. harass. v. pester, disturb, bother, annoy.

H11. hardly. adv.
scarcely, barely, only just, rarely.

H12. hardship. n.
misfortune, suffering, difficulty, burden.

H13. harm. n.
hurt, damage, injury
v. injure, hurt, spoil.
A: 1. benefit, blessing
2. help, heal.

H14. harmless. adj.
safe, inoffensive, mild, gentle. A: harmful.

H15. harsh. adj.
1. jarring, grating, strident (noise) 2. cruel, stern, unkind (treatment)
3. coarse, rough, bristly (texture).
A: 2. kind 3. soft.

H16. harvest. v.
gather, reap, pick, collect
n. crop, produce, yield.
A: v. plant, sow n. seed.

H17. haste. n. speed, swiftness, hurry.
A: slowness, delay (hasten; hastily).

H18. hate. v. loathe, despise, detest. A: love.

H19. haughty. adj.
arrogant, proud, disdainful, snobbish.
A: modest.

H20. haul. v. drag, lug, tow, pull. A: push.
H: hall.

H21. hazard. n.
danger, peril, risk, threat
v. venture, chance, dare.
A: n. safeguard
v. protect.

H22. headlong. adv.
head-first, impulsively,
recklessly.

H23. headstrong. adj.
wilful, stubborn,
obstinate, uncontrollable.

H24. heal. v.
1. cure, mend, recover,
recuperate 2. reconcile,
settle, pacify (heal
differences) A: 1. harm,
wound. H: heel.

H25. heap. n.
pile, stack, mound.

H26. hear. v. listen,
heed, understand.
H: here.

H27. heart. n. 1. body
pump 2. feelings,
emotion, soul (know in
your heart) 3. focus,
core, essence (heart of
the matter) 4. centre,
middle, inner part (heart
of the city). A: 3. side
issue 4. outskirts.

H28. heartless. adj.
cruel, callous, unfeeling,
pitiless. A: kind,
sympathetic.

H29. heave. v. 1. haul,
pull, lift, hoist 2. pant,
exhale, breathe heavily
(heave a sigh) 3.billow,
swell, surge, (waves
heaved). A: 1. lower.

H30. heavy. adj.
1. weighty 2. difficult,
strenuous (heavy work)
3. important,
burdensome (heavy
responsibilities) 4. sad,
depressed, melancholy
(heavy heart). A: 1. light
2. easy 4. light-hearted.

H31. hectic. adj.
frantic, excited, bustling.
A: serene.

H32. heed. v. take
notice of, be guided by.
A: ignore, disregard.

H

H33. height. n.
tallness, highness,
elevation. A: depth.

H34. heir. n.
inheritor, beneficiary.
H: air.

H35. help. v.
1. aid, assist, support
2. save, rescue.
A: 1. hinder, oppose.

H36. helpless. adj.
weak, powerless,
confused, dependent.

H37. hereditary. adj.
inherited, inbred, passed
on. A: acquired.

H38. heroic. adj.
brave, daring,
courageous, bold.
A: cowardly.

H39. hesitate. v.
pause, falter, waver.
A: decide.

H40. hide. v.
1. conceal, cover,
seclude 2. cover, screen,
disguise 3. lie low, keep
out of sight.
A: 1. reveal 3. discover.

H41. high. adj.
1. tall, lofty, towering
2. excessive, costly (high
prices) 3. important,
influential, eminent (high
rank) 4. elated, cheerful,
gay (high spirits)
A: 1. low 3. lowly.

H42. hike. v. ramble,
trek, tramp, walk.

H43. hinder. v. delay,
detain, obstruct, stall
(hindrance).

H44. hint. n.
1. clue, tip, indication
2. trace, tinge, speck
(hint of lemon in the
sauce) v. suggest, imply.
A: 2. abundance, surplus
v. declare.

H45. hire. v.
1. employ, engage
2. lease, let, rent,
charter. A: 1. fire,
dismiss. H: higher.

H46. hit. v. 1. strike, smack, knock
2. succeed, achieve (song hit number one)
3. collide, crash, bump (car hit the tree) 4. affect, influence, touch (the news hit everyone). A: 1. pat, parry 2. fail 3. miss.

H47. hoard. n. store, cache, stockpile.

H48. hold. v. 1. grasp, grip, enfold, carry
2. contain 3. restrain, control (hold your fire)
4. maintain, keep up, retain (hold on)
5. extend, reach (hold out),(hold back; hold up). A: 1. drop, release.

H49. hollow. n. depression, dent, hole, crater, valley
adj. 1. empty, vacant, void 2. muffled, dull (hollow sound) 3. insincere, false, expressionless (her words sounded hollow)
4. concave, sunken.
A: 1. bulge adj.
1. occupied; 3. sincere.

H50. honour. n.
1. decency, integrity, loyalty (a man of honour)
2. respect, pay tribute to, praise (honour the brave)
3. privilege, distinction (honour to meet you).

A:1. baseness
2. condemn, dishonour
3. insult.

H51. hop. v. spring, bound, skip, bob.

H52. horizontal. adj. level, flat, even, plane. A: vertical.

H53. horrify. v. frighten, shock, terrify. A: delight.

H54. horror. n. dread, aversion, terror, panic. A: attraction.

H55. hostile. adj.
1. opposed, attacking
2. aggressive, quarrelsome, unfriendly, cold. A: friendly, sympathetic.

H56. hover. v.
1. hang, float, fly
2. linger, hang about, loiter.
A: 1. sink 2. withdraw.

H57. hub. n. centre, axis, core, pivot.

H58. huddle. v.
1. cluster, crowd, press
2. snuggle, nestle, curl
up. A: 1. disperse
2. stretch out.

H59. hue. n. colour,
shade, tint, tone. H: hew.

H60. hug. v. embrace,
clasp, hold, cuddle.

H61. huge. adj.
enormous, vast, immense,
colossal. A: tiny.

H62. hulking. adj.
bulky, oversized, heavy,
powerful.

H63. hull. n. shell,
husk, skin, body of a ship.

H64. hum. n. drone,
buzz, whir, murmur.

H65. humble. adj.
modest, unassuming,
meek. A: arrogant.

H66. humid. adj.
muggy, sticky, moist,
clammy.

H67. humiliate. v.
shame, humble, embarrass,
disgrace. A: honour.

H68. humorous. adj.
funny, witty, amusing,
comical. A: solemn.

H69. hurdle. n.
obstacle, barrier,
hindrance, snag
v. jump, leap, vault.

H70. hurl. v.
throw, pitch, fling, toss.
A: catch.

H71. hurry. v. hasten,
accelerate, speed up,
rush. A: dawdle.

H72. hurt. v. 1. pain,
ache 2. wound, injure,
harm, damage. A: 1.
heal, sooth 2. help.

H73. hurtle. v. speed,
race, whiz, rush. A: crawl.

H74. hush. v. quiet,
quell, still, soothe.
A: rouse.

H75. hustle. v.
1. hurry, hasten, rush
2. jostle, shove, push.

H76. hygienic. adj.
disinfected, germ-free,
clean, sterilised.
A: contaminated, dirty.

H77. hypocrisy. n.
insincerity, dishonesty,
two-facedness.
A: sincerity. (hypocrite;
hypocritical).

H78. hysterical. adj.
1. uncontrollable,
frenzied, frantic
2. hilarious, uproarious.
A: composed.

I1. idea. n. thought, concept, plan, notion.

I2. ideal. adj. perfect, faultless, suitable n. archetype, objective, aim, inspiration.

I3. identical. adj. indistinguishable, duplicate, same. A: distinct, unlike.

I4. identify. v. recognise, pick out, verify, detect. A: mistake, confuse.

I5. idle. adj. 1. inactive, not working 2. lazy, loafing. A: 1. active 2. energetic. H: idol.

I6. ignite. v. set on fire, kindle, light. A: extinguish.

I7. ignorant. adj. uninformed, unaware, uneducated. A: well-informed, knowledgeable.

I8. ignore. v. disregard, overlook, snub, take no notice of. A: acknowledge, heed.

I9. ill. adj. 1. unwell, sick 2. harmful, bad, unlucky, evil (ill effects). A: 1. healthy 2. favourable.

I10. illegal. adj. unlawful, forbidden. banned. A: legal.

I11. illegible. adj. unreadable, indistinct. A: legible, clear.

I12. illuminate. v. 1. light up 2. explain, make clear. A: 1. darken 2. obscure.

I13. illusion. n. trick, delusion, deception, misconception, false belief. A: reality.

I14. illustrate. v. show, picture, represent.

I15. imaginary. adj. unreal, made-up, fanciful, mythical. A: real.

I16. imitate. v. copy, mimic, impersonate, duplicate.

I17. immature. adj.
1. unripe, unformed
2. childish, inexperienced.
A: mature.

I18. immediately. adv.
instantly, directly, at
once. A: later.

I19. immense. adj.
huge, vast, gigantic,
mammoth. A: tiny.

I20. immerse. v.
1. submerge, dip, dunk,
drench 2. absorbed,
involved (immersed in
your work).

I21. immigrate. v.
enter, move into, settle.
A: leave, emigrate.

I22. immoral. adj.
wrong, sinful, wicked,
corrupt.
A: moral, honourable.

I23. impact. n.
1. collision, crash, bump
2. effect, shock.

I24. impartial. adj.
fair, neutral, unbiased.
A: prejudiced.

I25. impassive. adj.
unemotional, unmoved,
unresponsive.
A: emotional.

I26. impatient. adj.
restless, eager, anxious,
intolerant. A: patient.

I27. impede. v. hinder,
obstruct, block, delay.
A: assist.

I28. impel. v. force,
cause, push, urge, goad.
A: restrain, curb.

I29. imperfect. adj.
incomplete, faulty,
marred. A: perfect.

I30. impertinent. adj.
rude, cheeky, insolent.
A: respectful.

I31. impetuous. adj.
hasty, rash, impulsive.
A: restrained, cautious.

I32. implement. n.
tool, utensil
carry out, get done.
A: v. neglect.

I33. implore. v.
beg, plead, beseech.
A: demand.

I34. imply. v. suggest, hint, infer, indicate.

I35. important. adj.
1. significant, essential, urgent, serious
2. distinguished, famous, influential (person).
A: 1. unimportant
2. minor.

I36. impose. v. force, inflict, dictate, levy.
A: lift, remove.

I37. impossible. adj. unattainable, unimaginable.
A: possible, probable.

I38. impression. n.
1. feeling, belief
2. effect, impact, imprint.

I39. impressive. adj. imposing, splendid, thrilling, outstanding.
A: uninspiring.

I40. improbable. adj. unlikely, doubtful, questionable. A: likely.

I41. impromptu. adj. unprepared, spontaneous, sudden, impulsive. A: planned.

I42. improve. v.
1. get better, recover
2. progress, advance, develop, enhance
A: 1. worsen
2. harm, damage.

I43. impure. adj.
1. unclean, polluted, infected 2. indecent, obscene, smutty.
A: 1. pure, clean
2. decent, wholesome.

I44. inaccessible. adj. isolated, cut off, unreachable.
A: accessible.

I45. inadequate. adj. lacking, insufficient, unsatisfactory.
A: adequate.

I46. incense. v. anger, enrage, inflame, madden
n. perfume, fragrance.

I47. incessant. adj. ceaseless, continuous, nonstop. A: interrupted.

I48. incident. n. happening, event, occurrence.

I49. incline. v.
1. slope, slant, tilt
2. tend, prefer, like, have a mind to (she was inclined to wear pink)
3. bend, lean.
A: 2. dislike.

I

150. include. v.
contain, involve, take in, comprise.
A: exclude, omit.

151. income. n.
earnings, pay, wages, salary. A: expense.

152. increase. v.
add to, enlarge, expand, extend. A: decrease.

153. indeed. adv.
truly, in fact, really.

154. indefinite. adj.
inexact, unclear, vague, uncertain. A: definite.

155. indelible. adj.
fixed, permanent.

156. independent. adj.
self-reliant, uncontrolled, unconnected.
A: dependent.

157. indestructible.
adj. unbreakable, durable, permanent.
A: destructible, perishable.

158. index. n.
alphabetical list, directory, catalogue, table.

159. indicate. v.
1. point to, show
2. symbolise, stand for, imply.

160. indignant. adj.
offended, angry, infuriated, resentful.
A: delighted.

161. individual. adj.
single, separate, different, distinct.
A: collective, general.

162. indulgent. adj.
easy-going, lenient, tolerant, permissive.
A: stern, intolerant.

163. industrious. adj.
hard-working, busy, diligent. A: lazy

164. inedible. adj.
uneatable.

165. inert. adj. lifeless, motionless, still, sluggish.
A: dynamic, alert.

166. inevitable. adj.
unavoidable, certain, sure.
A: avoidable, uncertain.

167. inexplicable. adj.
unexplainable, baffling,

puzzling, mysterious.
A: obvious.

168. inferior. adj.
1. junior, lower,
subordinate
2. cheap, substandard,
lesser.
A: 1. senior
2. superior, prime.

169. infinite. adj.
boundless, endless,
immeasurable, limitless.
A: finite.

170. infringe. v.
violate, overstep,
disobey, trespass.

171. ingenious. adj.
inventive, clever,
imaginative, creative.
A: unoriginal,
unresourceful.

172. ingredient. n.
part, component,
element.

173. initial. adj.
first, earliest, opening,
original.
A: last, final.

174. inject. v. force
into, insert, introduce.
A: eject.

175. inquisitive. adj.
curious, prying,
interested.
A: uninterested.

176. insane. adj.
mad, crazy, deranged.
A: sane.

177. insert. v. push in,
put in. A: extract.

178. inside. n. interior,
centre, middle.
A: exterior, outside.

179. insist. v.
1. maintain, urge, assert,
stress 2. demand,
command, enforce.
A: 1. deny 2. ask.

180. insolent. adj.
disrespectful, cheeky,
rude, impertinent.
A: polite, civil.

181. inspire. v.
stimulate, encourage,
motivate.
A: stifle, suppress.

182. install. v.
establish, put in, place.

183. instinct. n.
intuition, feeling,
tendency.

184. intact. adj.
complete, entire, whole.
A: damaged.

185. integrity. n.
honesty, uprightness,
honour, respectability.
A: corruption.

I

I86. intellect. n. mind, reason, understanding.

I87. intend. v. mean, aim, plan, propose.

I88. intense. adj.
1. strong, powerful, potent 2. earnest, passionate, eager.
A: 1. weak 2. casual, indifferent.

I89. interfere. v. intrude, meddle, intervene, interrupt.
A: help.

I90. intimate. adj.
1. close, familiar, dear
2. personal, private, confidential. A: 1. distant
2. open, known.

I91. intrepid. adj. bold, brave, daring, fearless.
A: timid.

I92. intricate. adj. complicated, detailed, involved. A: simple.

I93. intrigue. n. plot, scheme
v. fascinate, interest, attract.

I94. inundate. v. drown, engulf, flood, swamp.

I95. invent. v. create, make up, devise.

I96. invigorating. adj. refreshing, stimulating, strengthening.
A: weakening.

I97. invisible. adj. hidden, unseen.

I98. involve. v.
1. include, contain
2. affect, absorb, concern.

I99. irate. adj. furious, angry, indignant, irritated.

I100. irrelevant. adj. unconnected, unrelated, inapt.

I101. irritate. v.
1. inflame, chafe, make sore 2. annoy, irk, exasperate.
A: 1. ease 2. mollify.

I102. isolate. v. segregate, set apart, detach. A: unite.

I103. item. n. article, object, thing.

J1. jab. v.
poke, prod, dig.

J2. jagged. adj.
pointy, ragged, notched,
serrated. A: smooth.

J3. jar. n.
pot, bottle, crock
v. 1. jolt, jerk, shake,
rattle
2. disturb, unsettle, stun.
A: 2. soothe.

J4. jaunt. n. outing,
trip, excursion.

J5. jealous. adj.
envious, resentful,
covetous, possessive.

J6. jeer. v. mock,
taunt, sneer, ridicule.
A: applaud.

J7. jeopardise. v.
risk, imperil, endanger,
expose. A: secure.

J8. jest. n.
joke, wisecrack, quip.

J9. jilt. v. forsake,
abandon, dump, desert.

J10. jinx. n. curse,
spell, hex, charm.

J11. job. n.
1. employment,
profession, trade
2. work, task, duty,
chore.

J12. join. v.
1. connect, unite,
combine 2. stick, glue,
attach 3. enrol, enlist,
subscribe. A: 1. sever,
part 2. separate 3. resign.

J13. jolly. adj. merry,
gay, jovial. A: solemn.

J14. jot. v. write down,
scribble, note, record.

J15. journey. n.
trip, travel, outing,
expedition.

J16. joy. n. happiness,
gladness, delight.
A: sorrow.

J17. judge. v.
1. decide, determine,
conclude, deduce
2. examine, investigate,
referee, mediate, rule on.

J18. juicy. adj.
succulent, lush, dripping.
A: dry.

J19. jumble. n.
confusion, muddle,
medley, tangle. A: order.

J

J20. jump. v. 1. leap, vault, bound, spring 2. start, flinch 3. switch, change (jump from one topic to another).

J21. junction. n. connecting point, intersection, crossroads A: separation.

J22. junk. n. rubbish, waste, trash, castoffs.

J23. just. adj. 1. fair, impartial, unbiased, objective 2. honourable, upright, ethical. adv. 1. lately, not long ago 2. hardly, scarcely, narrowly. A: 1. adj. unjust 2. devious.

J24. juvenile. adj. youthful, young, immature, childish.

K

K1. keen. adj. 1. sharp, fine-edged (knife) 2. shrewd, clever, smart, intelligent (mind) 3. eager, impatient, enthusiastic (keen to go). A:1. blunt 2. obtuse 3. apathetic.

K2. keep. v. 1. retain, save, preserve 2. store, stow (keep it in the cupboard) 3. support, provide for 4. continue, carry on, remain, endure (keep on). A: 1. discard.

K3. key. n. 1. opener 2. clue, pointer, explanation 3. tone, pitch, note.

K4. kill. v. slaughter, destroy, murder, annihilate, slay. A: revitalise, spare.

K5. kind. adj. considerate, warm-hearted, charitable, gentle n. type, sort, brand, category.

K6. kit. n. equipment, gear, tools, uniform, supplies.

K7. knack. n. aptitude, skill, talent, expertise. A: ineptitude.

K8. knave. n. rascal, scoundrel, rogue. A: gentleman.

K9. knead. v. massage, mould, press, shape.

K10. knock. v. rap, tap, bang, thump, strike.

K11. knot. v. tie, bind, secure, lash n. 1. hitch, twist, braid 2. cluster, group, bunch (knot of onlookers) 3. gnarl, lump, bump.

K12. know. v. understand, comprehend, discern, recognise (know that face), remember (she knew her ten times table).

L1. labour. v. drudge, toil, work, effort. A: rest.

L2. lack. v. 1. need, require, want 2. fall short, miss, be inadequate.

L3. lag. v. dawdle, linger, drag behind. A: lead.

L4. lair. n. den, cave, hideout, sanctuary.

L5. lament. v. mourn, weep, grieve. A: rejoice.

L6. landscape. n. scenery, view, outlook, countryside.

L7. lane. n. track, footpath, narrow road, byway.

L8. languid. adj. weary, drooping, listless, sluggish. A: strong, energetic.

L9. lanky. adj. tall and thin, slender, bony, lean. A: burly, plump.

L

L10. lapse. n. 1. slip, oversight, blunder 2. decline, relapse, regression 3. interval, pause, gap.

L11. lash. v. 1. tie, bind, fasten 2. whip, flog, thrash.

L12. last. adj. final, concluding, farthest, ultimate v. continue, persist, remain, endure. A: adj. first v. stop, end, cease.

L13. late. adj. overdue, behind time, unpunctual. A: early.

L14. lavish. adj. extravagant, generous, plentiful, sumptuous A: meagre, stingy.

L15. lax. adj. careless, irresponsible, neglectful. A: scrupulous.

L16. layer. n. 1. level, tier, band 2. coat, film, skin.

L17. lead. v. 1. guide, conduct, precede, go before. 2. direct, head, control n. 1. dog's leash 2. cable, wire, flex. A: 1. trail.

L18. leap. v. jump, spring, hurdle, bound. A: walk.

L19. leave. v. 1. go away from, depart, set out 2. abandon, desert, forsake 3. put down, place, set down (leave them there) 4. drop, omit, eliminate (leave out). A: 1. arrive 2. stay, retain.

L20. legible. adj. readable, clear. A: illegible.

L21. leisure. n. free time, ease, recreation, rest. A: labour.

L22. lend. v. loan.

L23. length. n. reach, distance, span, extent. A: width, depth.

L24. lenient. adj. merciful, mild, easygoing, forgiving. A: harsh, stern.

L25. less. adj. smaller, fewer, reduced, not as much. A: more.

L26. lethal. adj. fatal, deadly, mortal, dangerous. A: harmless, healthful.

L27. lethargic. adj. languid, lazy, slow, torpid. A: vigorous.

L28. level. adj. even, flat, smooth, parallel, constant. A: uneven, slanted.

L29. liable. adj. 1. likely, prone, inclined 2. responsible, obligated. A: 1. unlikely 2. exempt.

L30. liberty. n. freedom, independence. A: slavery, tyranny.

L31. lie. v. 1. sprawl, recline, loll 2. falsify, fib, misrepresent 3. be found, belong, be placed (the answer lies in here). A: 2. verify.

L32. light. n. 1. illumination, brightness, glare 2. approach, aspect, viewpoint (examine in a new light) 3. match, lighter, flame (do you have a light?) A: 1. darkness, dimness.

L33. like. adj. similar, akin, resembling v. 1. enjoy, appreciate 2. be fond of, admire, esteem.

L34. limited. adj. bounded, defined, restricted. A: unlimited.

L35. link. v. connect, couple, associate, implicate. A: separate.

L36. lip. n. brim, brink, rim, verge.

L

L37. liquid. adj. fluid, flowing, runny, melted.
A: solid.

L38. literal. adj. exact, precise, accurate, truthful.
A: liberal, inexact.

L39. load. n. 1. cargo, freight 2. burden, weight, pressure v. fill, pack, pile. A: v. unload.

L40. loan. v. lend, advance, borrow.
A: return.

L41. loathe. v. hate, detest, dislike. A: adore.

L42. locate. v. 1. find, track down, search out · 2. settle, move to.

L43. lofty. adj.
1. tall, high, elevated
2. arrogant, aloof, condescending (manner)
A: 1. stunted 2. humble, friendly.

L44. lonely. adj.
1. solitary, friendless, forlorn, alone 2. isolated, remote, desolate.
A: accompanied.

L45. long. adj.
lengthy, extended, prolonged v. yearn, crave, desire.
A: adj. short.

L46. look. v. 1. watch, stare, see 2. appear, seem (you look happy) 3. face, overlook.
A: 1. miss, ignore.

L47. loom. v.
materialise, appear, emerge.

L48. loose. adj.adv. untied, unfastened, free, unattached.
A: tied, tethered.

L49. lost. adj.
1. missing, mislaid, vanished 2. astray, confused, disorientated.
A: 1. found 2. saved.

L50. lot. n. 1. many, much, a great deal 2. fortune, fate, destiny 3. straw, counter (draw lots) 4. part, share, proportion (your lot).

L51. loud. adj. 1. noisy, deafening, booming 2. gaudy, flashy, garish.

L52. lovable. adj. endearing, appealing, charming. A: detestable.

L53. loyal. adj. faithful, true, reliable, trustworthy. A: disloyal, false.

L54. luck. n. fortune, fate, chance. A: design.

L55. ludicrous. adj. absurd, ridiculous, silly, comical. A: sensible, serious.

L56. lull. v. soothe, calm, quieten n. pause, gap, hiatus, brief silence. A: v. excite n. flow.

L57. lunge. n. charge, thrust, jab. A: parry.

L58. lurch. v. pitch, roll, stagger, reel.

L59. lure. v. entice, tempt, seduce, beguile. A: repel.

L60. lurk. v. skulk, sneak, lie in wait.

L61. luscious. adj. delicious, succulent, juicy. A: sour, tasteless.

L62. lush. adj. flourishing, dense, green. A: sparse, barren.

L63. lust. v. crave, desire, covet. A: spurn.

L64. luxurious. adj. expensive, rich, grand, elegant. A: frugal, squalid.

M

M1. machine. n. mechanism, device, apparatus, appliance.

M2. mad. adj. 1. crazy, insane, demented 2. angry, furious, annoyed. A: 1. sane 2. appeased.

M3. made. adj. produced, built, manufactured, created.

M4. magic. n. witchcraft, sorcery, voodoo, enchantment.

M5. magnify. v. enhance, intensify, amplify, enlarge. A: minimise.

M6. maim. v. cripple, disable, injure, mutilate.

M7. main. adj. foremost, chief, leading, principal. A: secondary, lesser.

M8. maintain. v. 1. sustain, preserve, uphold, continue 2. keep, support, provide for 3. assert, declare, insist.

M9. majestic. adj. stately, noble, grand, imposing. A: ordinary, lowly.

M10. major. adv. 1. greater, larger (major part) 2. leading, capital, important, principal (major city). A: minor.

M11. make. v. 1. manufacture, produce, create 2. compel, force, oblige (make her go) 3. reach, achieve, attain (make the team) 4. bring about, establish, cause (make laws). A: 1. destroy 2. ask 3. miss 4. abolish.

M12. malice. n. spite, hate, ill will. A: goodwill.

M13. mall. n. promenade, walk, arcade, plaza.

M14. manage. v.
1. direct, supervise, govern 2. handle, control, operate 3. get on, fare, cope.

M15. manipulate. v.
1. control, handle, operate 2. influence, contrive, exploit 3. finger, feel, massage.

M16. manner. n.
1. way, style, method 2. behaviour, conduct, attitude.

M17. manoeuvre. n.
tactics, war plan, exercise
v. plan, scheme, ploy.

M18. manual. n.
instruction book, text-book, primer, directory.

M19. manufacture. v.
1. make, produce, assemble 2. fabricate, invent, concoct.
A: 1. demolish.

M20. many. adj.
numerous, various, countless.

M21. mar. v. spoil, deface, damage, mark.
A: enhance, restore.

M22. margin. n.
1. edge, border, fringe 2. room, leeway, space.

M23. marine. adj.
of the sea, nautical, naval, seagoing
A: terrestrial.

M24. marked. adj.
noticeable, distinct, outstanding, conspicuous.
A: commonplace.

M25. maroon. v.
strand, abandon, isolate, desert. adj. brownish red, wine. (N.B. chestnut-coloured, from French 'marron').

M26. marsh. n.
bog, fen, swamp.

M27. martial. adj.
militant, warlike, combative, soldierly (martial arts).

M28. marvel. n.
wonder, miracle, phenomenon, spectacle.

M29. mask. v. cover, disguise, conceal, screen.
A: reveal.

M

M30. mass. n.
1. matter, material, weight
2. block, lump, chunk
3. crowd, throng, group.

M31. massive. adj.
immense, huge, vast, colossal. A: tiny.

M32. masterly. adj.
expert, skilled, brilliant, clever. A: amateur.

M33. masterpiece. n.
classic, work of art, treasure.

M34. materialise. v.
appear, occur, come into being, emerge.
A: vanish.

M35. maternal. adj.
motherly, protective, nurturing, caring.
A: paternal.

M36. matter. n.
1. material, stuff, substance 2. topic, theme, subject 3. affair, situation, proceeding (heart of the matter) 4. importance, consequence, concern (of no matter) 5. problem, trouble, difficulty (what's the matter?).

M37. maul. v. mangle, injure, rough up, pound.

M38. maverick. n.
1. unbranded calf
2. individualist, nonconformist, dissenter.

M39. maxim. n.
proverb, truism, motto.

M40. maximum. adj.
greatest, most, highest, top. A: minimum.

M41. maybe. adv.
perhaps, possibly.

M42. maze. n.
labyrinth, network, complex.

M43. meagre. adj.
inadequate, scanty, mean, sparse. A: ample.

M44. mean. v.
1. intend, propose, want
2. signify, indicate, denote adj. 1. stingy, miserly 2. hardhearted, unkind, petty.
A: 2. conceal
3. generous
4. compassionate.

M45. meander. v.
1. wind, snake, zigzag
2. wander, ramble.

M46. measure. v.
1. size 2. evaluate,
assess, gauge.

M47. meddle. v.
interfere, intrude, pry.

M48. mediocre. adj.
average, passable,
middling, ordinary.

M49. meditate. v.
reflect, contemplate,
muse, focus on.

M50. meek. adj. mild,
tolerant, submissive.
A: domineering, bold.

M51. meet. v.
1. welcome, greet
2. encounter, confront,
run into 3. assemble,
gather 4. fulfil, observe,
obey (meet the
conditions). A: 2. avoid
3. adjourn, disperse
4. fall short of. H: meat.

M52. melancholy. adj.
unhappy, depressed,
despondent, glum.
A: joyful.

M53. mellow. adj.
1. ripe, mature,
full-flavoured 2. rich,
resonant, rolling (mellow
tones). A: 1. sour, unripe
2. discordant.

M54. melt. v.
1. dissolve, thaw
2. fade, vanish, dissipate
(crowd melted away).

M55. memorable. adj.
unforgettable, notable,
significant, historic.

M56. menace. n.
threat, danger, hazard.
A: advantage.

M57. mend. v.
1. repair, restore
2. darn, patch, sew
A: damage, ruin.

M58. menial. adj.
lowly, servile, ignoble.
A: dignified.

M59. mention. v. refer
to, comment on, cite.

M60. merciful. adj.
forgiving, lenient,
pitying, compassionate.
A: merciless.

M

M61. merge. v. blend, unite, amalgamate, join. A: diverge, separate.

M62. merit. n. worth, value, quality. A: worthlessness.

M63. merry. adj. jolly, cheerful, gleeful, laughing. A: gloomy.

M64. mess. n. 1. clutter, disorder, untidiness. 2. predicament, pickle, trouble.

M65. message. n. report, note, communication, statement.

M66. method. n. system, technique, way, style, routine.

M67. middle. adj. centre, mid-point, core, halfway, nucleus. A: edge.

M68. mighty. adj. 1. powerful, strong, forceful 2. massive, majestic, monumental.

M69. migrate. v. relocate, emigrate, journey.

M70. mild. adj. 1. gentle, placid, easygoing 2. warm, balmy, summery (weather). A: 1. fierce 2. stormy.

M71. mimic. v. imitate, copy, ape.

M72. mingle. v. mix, merge, blend, combine. A: divide.

M73. miniature. adj. small-scale, tiny, minute. A: enlarged.

M74. minimum. adj. least, smallest, lowest. A: maximum.

M75. minor. adj. trivial, petty, small, slight.

M76. miracle. n. wonder, marvel, mystery, phenomenon.

M78. mirage. n. illusion, unreality, hallucination.

M79. mirth. n. amusement, gaiety, laughter, hilarity. A: dejection.

M80. miscellaneous. adj. assorted, varied, mixed.

M81. miserable. adj.
1. unhappy, woeful, depressed, sad
2. wretched, poor, pitiable. A: 1. happy
2. respectable.

M82. mishap. n. accident, misfortune, disaster.

M83. mission. n. purpose, task, assignment, quest.

M84. mistake. n. error, blunder, fault, oversight.

M85. misty. adj. hazy, steamy, blurred, fuzzy. A: clear.

M86. moan. v. groan, grumble, complain.

M87. mob. n. pack, rabble, crowd, horde.

M88. mobile. adj. movable, travelling. A: permanent, static.

M89. moderate. adj. average, medium, middling, fair. A: extreme.

M90. modern. adj. contemporary, current, new, recent. A: antique.

M91. modest. adj. unassuming, humble, plain, shy, demure. A: vain, impudent.

M92. moist. adj. damp, wet, clammy, muggy, dank. A: dry.

M93. molest. v. harass, attack, assault, abuse, bother.

M94. moment. n.
1. instant, second, trice, flash 2. occasion, point in time (at this moment) 3. significance, importance (of no moment), (momentous).

M95. monopolise. v. control, dominate, take over. A: share.

M96. monotonous. adj. dull, dreary, boring, flat, colourless, toneless.

M

M97. moor. v.
berth, dock, tie up,
anchor n. heath,
moorland, fell. H: more.

M98. mope. v. sulk,
fret, brood, grieve.

M99. morbid. adj.
pessimistic, gloomy,
dour.

M100. more. adj.
extra, additional, other,
added. A: less. H: moor.

M101. motive. n.
reason, purpose,
intention.

M102. motley. adj.
unlike, varied, different.

M103. mound. n.
1. heap, pile, stack
2. ridge, knoll, dune.

M104. mount. v.
1. ascend, climb 2. rise,
go up, increase (prices
mounted) 3. fit, set into
(mount the picture).

M105. mourn. v.
grieve, pine, lament,
despair. A: rejoice.

M106. much. adj.
plenty, ample,
abundance.

M107. muffle. v.
1. swathe, envelop,
wrap up
2. stifle, deaden, hush.

M108. mundane. adj.
ordinary, commonplace,
day-to-day. A: heavenly.

M109. murmur. n.
whisper, undertone,
mumble, mutter.
A: shout.

M110. musty. adj.
mouldy, mildewed,
stale, fusty.

M111. mutilate. v.
maim, butcher, chop up,
dismember.

M112. mutual. adj.
joint, common,
interactive, reciprocated.

M113. myriad. adj.
countless, measureless,
untold.

M114. mysterious.
adj. inexplicable,
puzzling, strange,
baffling, unknown.
A: plain, apparent.

N1. naive. adj.
innocent, unworldly,
simple. A: sophisticated.

N2. naked. adj. nude,
unclothed, bare.

N3. nap. v. doze,
drowse, snooze, sleep.

N4. narrate. v.
describe, recite, recount,
(tell a story).

N5. narrow. adj.
1. slim, slender, thin
2. cramped, restricted,
small (narrow confines)
3. biased, prejudiced,
intolerant (narrow-
minded) A: 1. wide
2. spacious 3. liberal.

N6. nasty. adj.
unpleasant, disagreeable,
awful, mean.
A: nice, admirable.

N7. natural. adj.
normal, earthly, inherent,
regular, inborn.
A: unnatural, artificial,
assumed.

N8. naughty. adj.
disobedient, mischievous,
bad, misbehaving.
A: good.

N9. navigate. v.
1. sail, steer, pilot
2. voyage, cross, traverse.

N10. near. adv.
close, nearby, at hand.
A: distant, far.

N11. neat. adj.
tidy, orderly, trim,
uncluttered.
A: messy, untidy.

N12. necessary. adj.
needed, required,
essential, crucial.
A: optional.

N13. need. v.
require, want, lack, call
for n. poverty, distress,
suffering (in desperate
need).
A: n. excess, affluence.

N14. negative. adj.
1. refusing, opposing,
disagreeing
2. uncooperative,
unwilling, pessimistic
(negative attitude).
A: positive.

N15. neglect. v.
ignore, overlook, forget,
miss. A: attend, care.

N

N16. negotiate. v.
discuss, bargain, arrange,
settle.

N17. neighbourhood.
n. district, community,
parish, quarter.

N18. neighbouring.
adj. nearby, bordering,
next to, adjoining.
A: distant.

N19. nemesis. n.
destruction, ruin,
vengeance, justice.

N20. nerve. n.
courage, daring, pluck,
boldness.
A: faintheartedness.

N21. nestle. v.
snuggle, cuddle, huddle,
lie close.

N22. net. n.
1. mesh, web, lattice
2. snare, trap
v. 1. ensnare, catch, bag
2. earn, gain, collect.
H: nett.

N23. neutral. adj.
1. impartial, unbiased,
uninvolved
2. indefinite, toneless,
colourless (colour).
A: 1. involved, biased.

N24. nevertheless.
adv. however, anyhow,
regardless.

N25. new. adj.
1. modern, recent,
current 2. fresh, unused,
mint 3. untried, untested,
unfamiliar. A: 1. old-
fashioned, antique 2. old,
stale 3. familiar, reliable.

N26. next. adj.
1. following, after,
succeeding 2. closest,
nearest.

N27. niche. n. recess,
alcove, nook, cranny,
cubbyhole.

N28. nimble. adj. agile,
fast, lithe, spry.
A: clumsy, slow.

N29. noble. adj.
1. highborn, aristocratic,
princely
2. grand, majestic,
stately
3. upright, honourable,
worthy.
A: 1. lowly
2. modest, plain
3. base, vulgar.

N30. noise. n. sound, racket, clamour, uproar. A: silence.

N31. nominate. v. name, choose, propose, select.

N32. nonchalant. adj. unconcerned, blasé, unaffected. A: moved.

N33. nondescript. adj. ordinary, indistinctive.

N34. nonsense. n. foolishness, folly, rubbish, drivel. A: sense.

N35. normal. adj. average, common, usual, ordinary, expected. A: abnormal, unusual.

N36. notable. adj. obvious, noticeable, conspicuous, striking. A: vague, hidden.

N37. noted. adj. famous, well-known, distinguished, eminent. A: unknown.

N38. notify. v. tell, inform, advise, warn.

N39. notion. n. idea, belief, fancy, whim.

N40. novel. adj. new, different, unusual, original. A: usual, customary.

N41. novice. n. beginner, learner, apprentice. A: professional.

N42. nucleus. n. core, heart, centre. A: exterior.

N43. nude. adj. naked, bare, unclad.

N44. nuisance. n. annoyance, pest, bother, irritation. A: delight.

N45. null. adj. invalid, void, worthless, no-good. A: valid.

N46. numb. adj. unfeeling, senseless, deadened.

N47. numerous. adj. many, plentiful, lots. A: few.

N48. nurture. v. nourish, feed, care for, maintain. A: neglect.

N49. nymph. n. dryad, sylph, naiad.

O

O1. oath. n.
1. vow, promise, pledge
2. curse, swear-word.

O2. obedient. adj.
biddable, dutiful, law-abiding.
A: disobedient (obey).

O3. object. n.
1. purpose, goal, aim
2. thing, article, item
v. oppose, protest,
refuse. A: v. approve.

O4. obligation. n.
duty, responsibility,
commitment. A: choice.

O5. oblige. v.
1. force, make, demand
2. favour, help,
accommodate.
A: 1. persuade
2. inconvenience.

O6. obscure. adj.
unclear, unheard of, dim,
indefinite. A: clear.

O7. observant. adj.
watchful, alert, attentive,
interested.
A: unobservant.

O8. obsession. n.
fixed idea, passion,
mania, craze (obsessed).

O9. obsolete. adj.
dated, discontinued,
old-fashioned.

O10. obstacle. n.
barrier, obstruction,
block, snag.
A: spur, boon.

O11. obtain. v. get,
acquire, receive, come
by. A: lose.

O12. obvious. adj.
evident, clear, apparent,
plain.
A: concealed, obscure.

O13. occasionally.
adv. sometimes, now and
then, at times.
A: always (occasional).

O14. occupant. n.
resident, tenant,
inhabitant, dweller.

O15. occupation. n.
trade, profession, job,
business.

O16. occur. v.
1. happen, take place,
befall 2. arise, appear,
be found 3. suggest itself
to, come into one's head
(it occurs to me).

O17. odd. adj.
1. not even 2. strange, queer, uncommon
3. unmatched, left over, single. A: 1. even
2. ordinary 3. paired.

O18. odour. n.
smell, aroma, scent, fragrance, stench.

O19. offend. v.
displease, insult, hurt, affront. A: please, charm (offensive).

O20. offer. v.
1. present, extend, hold out 2. propose, submit, render, suggest (make an offer).

O21. often. adj.
frequently, repeatedly, regularly.
A: rarely, seldom.

O22. ogle. v. stare, gape, gawk, leer.

O23. old. adj.
1. elderly, aged, ancient
2. antiquated, out-of-date, obsolete

3. worn out, dilapidated, used. A:1.young 2,3 new.

O24. omen. n.
sign, token, warning.

O25. ominous. adj.
threatening, menacing, ill-omened.
A: favourable.

O26. omit. v.
leave out, exclude, miss, forget, overlook.
A: include, remember.

O27. once. adv.
1. one time
2. previously, in times past, formerly.
A: 1. never, frequently
2. hereafter.

O28. only. adv.
merely, just, simply.

O29. onward. adj.
forward, advancing, progressive. A: backward.

O30. ooze. v.
seep, trickle, drip, drain.
A: gush.

O

O31. open. adj.
1. not shut, ajar,
unfastened, unlocked
2. wide, unfenced (open
country) 3. impartial,
unbiased, just (open
mind) 4. sincere, artless,
natural (open person).
A: 1. closed, locked
2. crowded, bounded
3. biased, prejudiced
4. reserved.

O32. opening. n.
1. hole, gap, breach
2. launching, start,
beginning.
A: 1. obstruction
2. closing, finish.

O33. opponent. n.
rival, competitor, enemy
(oppose).

O34. oppressive. adj.
harsh, severe, unjust,
brutal. A: humane, kind.

O35. optimistic. adj.
cheerful, confident,
hopeful. A: pessimistic.

O36. option. n.
choice, alternative.

O37. opulence. n.
riches, wealth, luxury,
plenty. A: poverty, lack.

O38. ordeal. n.
trial, test, hardship.

O39. order. n.
1. command, instruction,
demand 2. system,
arrangement, grouping
3. quiet, calm, harmony
(restore order)
A: 1. request
2. confusion 3. chaos.

O40. ordinary. adj.
average, usual, normal,
commonplace,
humdrum.
A: extraordinary,
exceptional.

O41. organise. v.
1. set up, establish
2. arrange, classify,
categorise, tidy.
A: 1. disband 2. confuse.

O42. origin. n.
1. source, cause, reason,
basis 2. ancestry, family,
birth.

O43. original. adj.
1. earliest, first, initial
2. fresh, new, unusual,
imaginative.
A: 1. last 2. typical.

O44. other. adj.
additional, different,
opposite.

O45. outcast. n.
exile, fugitive, outlaw,
tramp.

O46. outcome. n.
result, effect,
consequence.

O47. outcry. n.
protest, uproar, clamour.

O48. outing. n. trip,
drive, excursion, jaunt.

O49. outlet. n.
opening, exit, channel,
duct.

O50. outline. n.
1. profile, silhouette,
contour, shape
2. sketch, drawing.

O51. outrage. n.
atrocity, scandal,
offence.

O52. outside. n.
1. exterior, surface,
covering
2. remote, slight
(outside chance)
A: 1. inside
2. certainty.

O53. outspoken. adj.
blunt, direct, frank.
A: tactful.

O54. outstanding. adj.
remarkable, exceptional.
distinguished,
A: ordinary.

O55. outwit. v. thwart,
outsmart, baffle, trap.

O56. over. adj.
done, finished, ended,
settled, gone 1. adv.
from top to bottom (all
over) 2. again, once
more, anew, often
3. remaining (left over).

O57. overdue. adj.
late, behind time.

O58. overhaul. v.
repair, service, inspect.

O59. overlook. v.
1. forget, miss, skip
2. ignore, disregard,
excuse 3. face, look on.

O60. oversight. n.
mistake, blunder,
inattention.

O61. own. v. have,
possess, hold.

P

P1. pace. n. 1. step, stride 2. rate, speed v. walk, amble, stroll. A: trot, run.

P2. pack. n. 1. parcel, bundle, package 2. group, herd, crowd v. fill, stuff, cram. A: v. unpack.

P3. pain. n. 1. ache, hurt, soreness 2. suffering, torment, ordeal, anguish. A: 1. comfort, relief 2. delight, pleasure. H: pane.

P4. pal. n. friend, mate, comrade. ('brother' in the Gypsy language. Romany)

P5. pale. adj. 1. ashen, white, wan (person) 2. light-coloured, toneless 3. dim, faint, indistinct (pallid; pallor) n. post, stake, picket. A: 1. ruddy, rosy 2. bright, vivid 3. clear, distinct. H: pail. .

P6. paltry. adj. measly, insignificant, trivial, petty. A: valuable, significant, grand.

P7 pamper. v. spoil, indulge, cosset. A: mistreat, abuse.

P8. panic. n. alarm, fear, hysteria, terror.

P9. parched. adj. dry, barren, lifeless. A: fertile.

P10. pardon. v. forgive, absolve, excuse, reprieve. A: punish, condemn.

P11. pare. v. peel, skin, trim, shave. A: increase, enlarge. H: pear; pair.

P12. partial. adj. 1. incomplete, unfinished 2. prejudiced, biased, interested. A: 1. complete, whole 2. impartial.

P13. particle. n.
speck, atom, fragment,
scrap.

P14. particular. adj.
1. specific, especial,
distinct 2. demanding,
fussy, critical.
A: 1. general, undefined
2. easy to please,
indifferent.

P15. pass. v. 1. go by,
proceed 2. elapse (time)
3. succeed, qualify
(exam) 4. hand over,
give, throw (pass the ball)
5. go beyond, surpass,
exceed (pass the speed
limit) n. 1. gorge, gap,
route 2. ticket, permit
(travel pass) 3. plight,
predicament, difficulty
(come to a pretty pass!)
A: 1. stop, withdraw,
retreat 3. fail 4. keep,
retain 5. fall behind,
pull back

P16. passion. n.
emotion, feeling, fervour,
enthusiasm. A: apathy,
coolness, indifference.
(passionate).

P17. pastime. n.
hobby, recreation,
diversion, activity.

P18. pathetic. adj.
pitiful, moving, touching,
distressing.
A: amusing, comical.

P19. patience. n.
tolerance, endurance,
calmness. A: impatience,
irritation. H: patients.

P20. pause. n.
break, interval, gap
v. 1. halt, hesitate, rest,
wait. A: n. continuity
v. continue. H: paws.

P21. peaceful. adj.
tranquil, quiet, serene,
untroubled. A: violent,
disturbed, noisy.

P22. peal. n. ring,
clang, knell. H: peel.

P23. peculiar. adj.
1. distinctive, unique,
special 2. odd, queer,
strange. A: 1. common
2. ordinary.

P

P24. penalty. n.
fine, punishment, forfeit.
A: reward.

P25. penitent. adj.
sorry, remorseful,
apologetic.
A: unrepentant.

P26. pensive. adj.
thoughtful, day-
dreaming, musing,
reflective.
A: carefree, frivolous.

P27. perceive. v.
discern, notice, detect,
apprehend. A: overlook,
ignore (perceptive,
perception).

P28. perfect. adj.
1. faultless, exact,
accurate 2. entire,
undamaged.
A: 1. faulty, flawed
2. incomplete, spoiled.

P29. perfume. n.
scent, fragrance, aroma.

P30. perhaps. adv.
maybe, possibly.

P31. peril. n. danger,
risk, threat, jeopardy.
A: safety.

P32. period. n. time,
interval, age, era, term.

P33. perish. v. die,
expire, decay, become
extinct. A: flourish.

P34. permanent. adj.
forever, lasting, constant,
perpetual. A: temporary,
impermanent.

P35. permission. n.
consent, approval,
agreement, authorisation
A: refusal, denial.
(permissible; permit).

P36. persecute. v.
torment, harass,
oppress, bully.
A: support, indulge.

P37. persist. v. keep
on, continue, endure,
maintain effort. A: quit.

P38. personal. adj.
1. individual, private,
confidential 2. insulting,
offensive, intrusive
(personal remarks).
A: impersonal, general.

P39. personnel. n.
employees, staff,
workers. H: personal.

P40. persuade. v.
convince, coax, induce,
win over. A: discourage.

P41. pester. v. bother,
annoy, harass, bait.

P42. petty. adj. trivial,
unimportant, minor,
small. A: important.

P43. phantom. n.
ghost, apparition,
spectre, illusion.

P44. phase. n.
1. stage, period, step
2. aspect, facet, feature.

P45. phenomenal. adj.
extraordinary,
exceptional, remarkable.
A: ordinary.

P46. phenomenon. n.
1. occurrence,
happening, event
2. wonder, marvel,
sensation.

P47. phobia. n.
unreasonable fear,
terror, dread.
A: liking, fondness.

P48. phony. adj. fake,
false, bogus, pseudo.
A: authentic, genuine.

P49. physical. adj.
1. bodily, of the body
2. material, existing,
solid.
A: spiritual, intangible.

P50. pierce. v.
puncture, penetrate, pass
through, perforate.

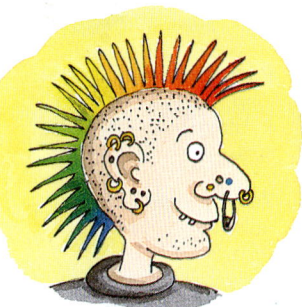

P51. piercing. adj.
1. shrill, loud, ear-
splitting (noise) 2. keen,
sharp, penetrating,
searching (glance).
A: 1. low, melodic
2. vague.

P52. pile. n. 1. heap,
stack, mound 2. nap,
surface, plush (carpet
pile) 3. post, support,
pillar.

P

P53. pinch. v.
1. tweak, nip, squeeze
2. arrest 3. steal
n. 1. speck, trace, bit
(pinch of salt)
2. discomfort, hardship,
plight (feel the pinch).

P54. pine. v. 1. yearn,
long, hanker after
2. mope, mourn, waste
away, die.

P55. pit. n. crater,
hole, cavity, hollow.
A: mound.

P56. pitch. v. 1. throw,
hurl, toss (a ball) 2. erect,
put up (tent) 3. rock,
lurch, shake (pitch about)
4. fall, topple, tumble
(pitch forward)
n. 1. incline, slope, angle
2. tone, sound (high
pitch) 3. level, degree,
measure (pitch of
excitement).

P57. pitiful. adj.
pathetic, heart-breaking,
distressing.

P58. pitiless. adj.
merciless, heartless,
callous.
A: compassionate.

P59. pity. n.
compassion, sympathy,
mercy, kindness.
A: apathy, inhumanity.

P60. placid. adj. calm,
serene, unruffled.
A: agitated.

P61. plain. adj.
1. clear, distinct, obvious
2. undecorated
3. unattractive, homely
4. blunt, direct, frank
(plain speaking)
A: 1. indistinct, obscure
2. fancy
3. beautiful, handsome
4. indirect. H: plane.

P62. plan. n.
1. blueprint, map,
diagram 2. scheme,
method, strategy
3. idea, aim, intention.

P63. plea. n. appeal,
request, entreaty (plead).

P64. pledge. n.
promise, assurance,
guarantee, word.

P65. pliable. adj.
flexible, bendable,
supple. A: stiff, rigid.

P66. plight. n.
situation, difficulty,
predicament, dilemma.

P67. pluck. v. pick,
pull off, extract, harvest
n. courage, grit, nerve.

P68. plunge. v.
1. dive, plummet, fall,
leap 2. immerse, dip,
thrust 3. charge, hurtle,
rush (plunge into the
crowd). A: 1. rise,
emerge 3. stroll, amble.

P69. plush. adj.
luxurious, elegant, posh.
A: tawdry.

P70. ply. n. layer,
thickness, sheet 1. v.
use, employ, operate,
2. carry on, follow (ply a
trade) 3. shower, heap,
lavish, thrust upon.

P71. point. n.
1. tip, apex, sharp end
2. object, aim, purpose
(what's the point?)
3. sense, reason, value
(no point to this)
4. location, position,
situation (point on map).
(pointless).

P72. poise. n.
assurance, confidence,
composure, balance.

P73. poke. v.
prod, jab, dig, thrust.

P74. polite. adj.
courteous, well-
mannered, respectful,
diplomatic. A: rude, ill-
mannered, crude.

P75. pollute. v.
dirty, contaminate, foul.
A: cleanse, purify.
(pollution).

P76. ponder. v.
think, consider, meditate,
contemplate.

P77. ponderous. adj.
heavy, bulky,
cumbersome, unwieldy.
A: light, dainty.

P

P78. portable. adj.
movable, compact,
lightweight, small.

P79. pose. v.
1. position, arrange
2. show-off
3. impersonate 4. ask,
put forward, present
(pose a question).

P80. positive. adj.
1. sure, convinced,
definite, certain
2. constructive,
progressive, helpful
(positive ideas).
A: 1. unsure 2. negative,
useless.

P81. possess. v.
own, hold, have, occupy.

P82. possible. adj.
achievable, obtainable,
feasible, likely.

P83. postpone. v.
defer, put off, delay.

P84. potential. adj.
likely, possible, probable.

P85. pounce. v.
swoop down, fall upon,
lunge at, jump at.

P86. pound. v. 1. beat,
pummel, hammer
2. throb, pulsate
3. pulverise, crush,
smash.

P87. power. n.
1. ability, talent, skill
2. strength, force, might,
energy 3. authority,
right, influence.
A: 1. incapacity
2. weakness.

P88. practice. n.
1. training, rehearsal,
repetition
2. custom, habit, routine
3. action, operation.

P89. precaution. n.
protection, safeguard,
defence.

P90. precious. adj.
valuable, expensive,
priceless, cherished.

P91. precise. adj.
exact, accurate, specific.
A: vague, inexact.

P92. predict. v.
foresee, foretell, forecast,
prophesy (prediction).

P93. prefer. v. like better, choose, fancy. A: dislike, detest.

P94. prejudice. n.
1. bias, preconception, prejudgment
2. intolerance, discrimination, closed-mindedness.

P95. premeditated. adj. planned, deliberate, intentional, calculated.

P96. premonition. n. warning, omen, indication, foreboding.

P97. preoccupied. v. absorbed, engrossed, busy, wrapped up in.

P98. preserve. v. keep safe, protect, save, conserve, maintain.

P99. presume. v. assume, deduce, suppose, guess.

P100. prevent. v. stop, hinder, deter, thwart, avert. A: permit, encourage.

P101. pride. n.
1. pleasure, satisfaction
2. self-respect, honour
3. conceit, self-importance, arrogance, vanity. A: 3. humility, modesty (proud).

P102. principal. adj. leading, foremost, chief, main n. Head. H: principle.

P103. principle. n.
1. rule, law, truth, maxim
2. ethics, honour, integrity.

P104. procedure. n. method, system, process, technique.

P105. proceed. v. continue, carry on, go on. A: stop, retreat.

P106. proceeds. n. profit, income, takings.

P107. progress. v. advance, improve, proceed. A: regress.

P108. project. n.
1. task, assignment, activity
2. plan, proposal, scheme
v. 1. extend, protrude, stick out
2. forecast, calculate, outline
3. show on screen.

P

P109. promise. n.
vow, oath, pledge, word.

P110. promote. v.
1. upgrade, raise
2. advertise, publicise.

P111. prompt. adj.
instant, immediate,
punctual, quick
v. 1. remind
2. spur, impel, inspire.

P112. prone. adj.
1. flat, horizontal, face-
down 2. inclined, liable,
apt. A: 1. vertical
2. unwilling.

P113. prosper. v.
do well, flourish, be
successful, thrive.
A: lose, grow poor.
(prosperous).

P114. protect. v.
guard, defend, shelter.
A: attack.

P115. protest. v.
object, complain,
oppose, demonstrate.
A: agree, approve.

P116. prove. v.
verify, demonstrate,
show, establish.
A: disprove, refute.

P117. provide. v.
give, supply, furnish,
equip. A: withhold,
deprive. (provision).

P118. provoke. v.
1. anger, annoy,
aggravate 2. incite,
cause, prompt. A: pacify.

P119. prowl. v. slink,
skulk, steal, roam.

P120. pry. v.
1. meddle, interfere,
snoop 2. lever, force,
jemmy (pry open).

P121. psychic. adj.
mental, psychological,
extrasensory,
supernatural.

P122. public. adj.
common, general,
shared, open. A: private.

P123. pull. v. haul,
tug, drag, tug, tow.
A: push.

P124. purpose. n.
objective, aim, intention,
goal, plan (purposeful,
purposely).

P125. pursue. v.
chase, follow, track, trail.
(pursuit).

P126. puzzle. v. baffle,
perplex, mystify, nonplus.

Q1. quail. v. cower, quake, tremble n. bird.

Q2. quaint. adj. old-fashioned, picturesque, antiquated, charming. A: modern.

Q3. qualify. v.
1. measure up, deserve, make the grade 2. train, prepare, make fit.

Q4. quality. n.
1. feature, aspect, trait, characteristic 2. value, worth, calibre
3. rank, distinction, status (man of quality).
A: 3. inferiority.

Q5. qualm. n.
uncertainty, doubt, misgiving, reluctance.
A: willingness.

Q6. quantity. n.
amount, number, measure, volume, mass.

Q7. quarrel. n.
argument, disagreement, dispute v. argue, bicker, wrangle, row.
A: n. agreement, harmony v. agree.

Q8. quay. n. wharf, dock, pier, jetty.

Q9. queer. adj. peculiar, abnormal, odd, unusual.
A: normal, ordinary.

Q10. quell. v. crush, subdue, suppress, quash. A: encourage, foster.

Q11. quest. n. search, hunt, journey, crusade.

Q12. quick. adj.
1. swift, rapid, fast
2. bright, intelligent, clever (quick-witted)
3. abrupt, sudden, hasty (quick end). A: 1. slow
2. dull 3. lingering.

Q13. quit. v.
1. leave, depart, withdraw
2. stop, cease, give up.
A: 1. arrive, remain
2. start, continue.

Q14. quite. adv.
totally, completely, entirely, wholly.

Q15. quota. n.
portion, share, ration.

R

R1. rabble. n. mob, crowd, gang, horde.

R2. racket. n. din, clamour, commotion, uproar.
A: silence, peace.

R3. radiant. adj.
1. shining, glowing, dazzling 2. happy, elated, overjoyed.
A: 1. sunless, overcast 2. sombre, sorrowful (radiance).

R4. rage. n. 1. wrath, anger, fury 2. fashion, craze, trend v. 1. rant, rave, roar 2. continue, go on (war raged).
A: n. 1. calmness.

R5. raise. v.
1. elevate, lift 2. build, construct 3. grow, produce, breed, rear (crop/family)
4. stimulate, arouse, stir up (raise hopes)
5. increase, inflate (raise prices) 6. collect, earn, make (raise money).

A: 1. lower 2. demolish, raze 4. quash, quell
5. reduce. H: raze; rays.

R6. rambling. adj. roundabout, circuitous, long-winded, wandering.
A: concise, direct (ramble).

R7. random. adj. haphazard, chance, irregular, occasional, unplanned. A: planned.

R8. range. n.
1. scope, selection, variety 2. chain, line (mountain range)
3. reach, limit, scope, extent
4. grazing land, pasture.

R9. rapid. adj. swift, speedy, fast, hasty.
A: slow.

R10. rare. adj. scarce, uncommon, unfamiliar, exceptional. A: common.

R11. rash. adj. reckless, thoughtless, impulsive, hasty.

R12. rate. n. 1. speed, pace, tempo 2. charge, price, fare, tariff.

R13. ravage. v. ruin, devastate, wreck, destroy.

R14. rave. v. 1. babble, ramble 2. rant, rage, fume 3. be enthusiastic.

R15. ravenous. adj. famished, greedy, hungry, starving. A: satiated.

R18. real. adj. 1. actual, authentic, genuine (real fur) 2. true, factual, certain (real facts) 3. sincere, honest, pure (real love) A: 1. fake 2. untrue 3. feigned.

R19. realise. v. apprehend, grasp, comprehend, see, understand.

R20. rear. n. back, end, tail, posterior, stern v. raise, nurture, bring up.

R16. raw. adj. 1. uncooked, rare 2. natural, crude, unprocessed 3. sore 4. frank, plain (raw facts) 5. cold, bitter, bleak (raw weather).

R17. reach. v. 1. arrive at, get to 2. extend, stretch (reach out) 3. grab, grasp, touch (reach for) 4. contact, find (reach me at).

R21. reason. n. 1. cause, motive, explanation 2. intelligence, judgment, sense (use your reason) 3. common sense, logic (listen to reason) v. consider, think, debate.

R22. rebel. v. disobey, mutiny, revolt, riot. (rebellious, rebellion).

R

R23. rebuke. v.
reprove, scold, lecture,
blame. A: praise.

R24. recede. v. go
back, ebb, regress, abate,
fade away. A: advance.

R25. receive. v.
1. get, acquire, obtain
2. entertain, greet,
welcome (receive visitors)
3. hear, learn, be told
(receive news)
4. encounter,
experience, undergo
(receive punishment).
(reception).

R26. receptacle. n.
container, box, bin,
holder.

THIS
WAY
UP

R27. reckless. adj.
rash, heedless,
incautious, careless.
A: cautious.

R28. recognise. v.
1. know, identify, pick
out, recall 2. appreciate,
understand, realise
3. discern, distinguish,
see. A: 2. ignore.

R29. reconcile. v.
reunite, arbitrate, mend,
conciliate, make up.

R30. recover. v.
1. get back, retrieve,
recoup, regain
2. get well, heal, mend.

R31. recur. v. come
again, repeat, return,
reappear.

R32. reduce. v.
1. lessen, decrease, cut,
diminish 2. cheapen,
mark down 3. diet, slim,
lose weight 4. degrade,
disgrace, demote.
A: 1. increase 2. inflate
4. promote, elevate.

R33. reek. n.
stink, stench, odour.

R34. refine. v.
filter, purify, cleanse.
A: contaminate.

R35. reform. v. correct,
improve, change, restore.

R36. refuge. n.
shelter, sanctuary,
protection, haven.

R37. refund. v.
repay, return, reimburse
A: withhold.

R38. refurbish. v.
renew, redo, restore,
renovate.

R39. refuse. v. reject, decline, forbid, turn down. A: accept, allow.

R40. regal. adj. royal, lordly, majestic, stately, grand.

R41. regard. v.
1. look, contemplate, gaze 2. consider, think, believe 3. heed, follow, accept (regard this advice).
A: disregard 3. reject.

R42. region. n. area, zone, district, territory.

R43. regret. n. remorse, sorrow, grief, rue. A: contentment.

R44. regular. adj.
1. consistent, periodic, recurring, frequent 2. even, uniform, symmetrical (regular features) 3. usual, habitual, customary (regular habit)
A: 1. irregular 2. uneven 3. occasional

R45. reign. v. rule, govern, command.
H: rein; rain.

R46. reject. v. refuse, rebuff, dismiss, decline.
A: accept, receive.

R47. rejoicing. n. celebration, revelry, merriment, delight (rejoice).

R48. relate. v.
1. tell, describe, recount 2. connect, link, associate.
A: separate, disconnect.

R49. relevant. adj. linked, connected, related. A: irrelevant.

R50. reliable. adj. dependable, responsible, trustworthy, efficient.
A: unreliable.

R51. relieve. v.
1. ease, reassure, lessen, comfort 2. assist, aid 3. replace, release.
A: 1. aggravate, alarm 2. burden, oppress.

R

R52. relinquish. v.
give up, hand over,
renounce, surrender.
A: keep, sustain.

R53. relish. v. enjoy,
delight in, appreciate.

R54. reluctant. adj.
unwilling, hesitant,
disinclined.
A: keen, eager.

R55. rely. v.
depend, count on, trust.

R56. remain. v.
stay, continue, linger,
persist, survive.

R57. remark. n.
comment, observation,
word
v. comment, observe,
mention

R58. remedy. n.
cure, treatment,
medicine v. 1. cure, heal
2. fix, correct.
A: 2. intensify 3. worsen.

R59. remiss. adj.
careless, lax, unthinking,
negligent. A: careful.

R60. remit. v. 1. pay,
send, forward, 2. forgive,
pardon, excuse 3. free,
release, liberate.
A: 1. withhold
2. condemn, punish
3. imprison.

R61. remorse. n.
regret, shame, sorrow.
A: satisfaction.

R62. remote. adj.
1. distant, far-off,
isolated, solitary 2. slight,
doubtful, unlikely (remote
possibility). A: 1. nearby
2. likely, attainable.

R63. renovate. v.
renew, repair,
modernise, remodel.

R64. rent. n.
rental, payment, fees
v. charter, hire.

R65. repel. v.
1. push back, repulse,
keep out, resist 2.
disgust, revolt, sicken.
A: 1. attract 2. delight.

R66. replica. n.
copy, duplicate,
imitation, reproduction.

R67. reply. v.
answer, respond, retort.
A: question, ask.

R68. report. n.
1. account, description
2. article, record, statement
3. noise, detonation, boom.

R69. repulsive. adj.
offensive, disgusting, ugly, hideous.
A: attractive, tasteful.

R70. repute. n.
renown, fame, respect, name (reputation, reputable).

R71. require. v.
1. need, want, lack
2. order, command, compel. A: forgo.

R72. resolve. v.
determine, decide, intend (resolute).

R73. respectable. adj.
1. decent, honest, honourable
2. presentable, modest, refined.

R74. respond. v. reply, answer, react.

R75. responsible. adj.
1. reliable, sensible, trustworthy, capable
2. guilty (responsible for the crime)
3. accountable, in charge of.

R76. rest. n.
1. extra, surplus, remainder
2. break, pause, lull
3. ease, leisure, relaxation 4. stand, support (book rest)
5. standstill, halt (came to rest).

R77. restrict. v. confine, restrain, curb, limit.

R78. result. n. effect, consequence, solution, outcome. A: cause.

R79. retreat. n.
1. escape, flight, withdrawal, getaway
2. refuge, hideaway, haven, sanctuary.
A: advance.

R80. retrieve. v.
recover, regain, reclaim, fetch.

R81. return. v.
1. come back, go back, reappear 3. give back, restore, put back.

R82. reverberate. v.
echo, rumble, resound, vibrate.

R

R83. reverse. adj. opposite, backward, inverted n.1. opposite, contrary 2. back, rear, other side v. 1. turn over, turn around, go backwards 2. undo, countermand (reverse a decision). A: n. 2. front v. 2. uphold.

R84. revise. v. 1. correct, alter, rewrite, modify, update 2. learn, study.

R85. revive. v. rouse, freshen, resuscitate, renew.

R86. revolve. v. turn around, rotate, spin, twirl, gyrate.

R87. reward. n. prize, payment, award, compensation.

R88. rhythm. n. beat, tempo, flow, emphasis, movement.

R89. rich. adj. 1. wealthy, affluent, well-off (person) 2. luxurious, precious, costly (possessions) 3. intense, deep, vivid (colour). A: 1. poor, destitute.

R90. rid. v. free, clear, remove.

R91. ridicule. v. mock, insult, sneer, belittle. A: praise, respect.

R92. ridiculous. adj. absurd, foolish, comical, bizarre.

R93. rift. n. crack, split, cleft, break.

R94. righteous. adj. moral, honest, honourable, just. A: bad, wicked.

R95. rigid. adj. 1. stiff, fixed, hard, unbending 2. strict, stern, stubborn, narrow-minded. A: 1. flexible, supple 2. lenient, tolerant.

R96. rim. n.
brim, edge, brink, lip.

R97. riot. n. anarchy,
mutiny, disorder, revolt.

R98. rip. v.
tear, split, rend, slash.

R99. ripe. adj.
mature, mellow,
blooming, seasoned.
A: unripe, green.

R100. rise. v.
1. stand, get up
2. rebel, revolt, disobey
(rise against)
3. ascend, go up
4. increase, escalate,
enlarge, swell
5. slope, slant upward.
A: 1. sit, lie down
3. descend
4. fall, decrease.

R101. risk. n.
1. danger, hazard
2. chance, gamble,
venture. (risky)

R102. rival. n. enemy,
opponent, contestant.
A: ally, helper.

R103. roam. v. travel,
ramble, range, wander.

R104. robust. adj.
hardy, healthy, strong,
fit. A: weak, sickly.

R105. rogue. n.
scoundrel, villain,
troublemaker, con man.

R106. role. n.
part, job, task, position,
character.

R107. romantic. adj.
1. sentimental,
emotional, passionate
2. unrealistic, fanciful,
idealised (romance).

R108. room. n.
1. chamber,
compartment
2. space, scope, leeway.

R109. root. n. 1. bulb,
tuber 2. base, foundation
3. origin, source, motive.

R110. rotten. adj.
1. decaying, putrid, bad
2. dishonest, corrupt,
wicked.

R

R111. rough. adj.
1. unsmooth, coarse, bumpy, jagged 2. harsh, difficult, unpleasant (rough time) 3. uncouth, vulgar, impolite (rough manners) 4. stormy, wild, wintry (rough weather). A: 1. smooth 2. easy 3. refined 4. balmy.

R112. routine. n. practice, custom, method, system.

R113. rub. v.
1. polish, wipe, buff 2. massage, stroke, knead.

R114. rubbish. n. trash, refuse, garbage, junk, litter.

R115. rude. adj. impolite, impudent, cheeky, crude, insolent. A: polite, civil.

R116. rue. v. regret, repent n. remorse, sorrow, shame.

R117. rugged. adj. rough, uneven, rocky, craggy.

R118. ruins. n. debris, remains, shell, wreckage.

R119. rule. n.
1. law, order, regulation 2. code, guideline, formula 3. practice, custom, routine.

R120. rummage. v. poke around, search, ransack, disarrange.

R121. rumour. n. supposition, gossip, hearsay.

R122. rupture. v. burst, break, split.

R123. ruse. n. trick, deception, manoeuvre, ploy.

R124. rustic. adj. rural, country, simple, unrefined.

R125. rut. n.
1. furrow, groove, track 2. dull routine, pattern, habit.

R126. ruthless. adj. merciless, pitiless, cruel, heartless, brutal.

S1. safe. adj.
1. secure, unharmed
2. protected, guarded,
unexposed 3. reliable,
dependable.
A: unsafe (safety).

S2. sake. n. good,
benefit, consideration,
welfare (for my sake).

S3. sallow. adj.
yellowish, wan, pale,
sickly.

S4. salvage. v. rescue,
save, recover, retrieve.

S5. sample. n.
example, specimen,
pattern, representation,
taste, hand-out.

S6. satisfy. v.
1. content, please
2. fill, quench, satiate
3. convince, reassure
(answer satisfied her).
A: dissatisfy, worsen
(satisfactory, satisfaction)

S7. saturate. v.
drench, soak, douse.
A: dry.

S8. saunter. v. stroll,
amble, walk, wander.

S9. savage. adj.
1. untamed, wild
2. primitive, uncivilised
3. ferocious, fierce,
brutal.
A: 1. tame 2. cultured
3. gentle, merciful.

S10. save. v. 1. rescue,
deliver 2. reserve, keep,
store 3. protect, preserve,
maintain (save the
planet). A: 2. use, waste
3. expose, endanger.

S11. scamper. v. run,
scurry, hurry, dart.

S12. scan. v.
1. skim, glance through
(scan the chapter)
2. examine, study, inspect
(scan the evidence).

S13. scandalous. adj.
disgraceful, shameful,
outrageous.
A: proper. (scandal).

S14. scanty. adj.
limited, meagre,
inadequate, skimpy,
mean.
A: ample, plentiful.

S

S15 scarcely. adj.
hardly, barely, only just.

S16. scare. v. frighten,
terrify, startle, shock.
A: reassure (scary).

S17. scatter. v.
disperse, strew, sprinkle,
sow.

S18. scene. n.
1. setting, site, location,
place 2. view, outlook,
landscape 3. fuss,
commotion, disturbance
(Tom made a scene).
H: seen.

S19. schedule. n.
agenda, list, programme,
timetable.

S20. scheme. n.
1. plan, method, system
2. plot, secret plan.

S21. scope. n.
range, extent, limit.

S22. scorch. v.
singe, sear, char, toast.

S23. scorn. n.
contempt, disdain, ridicule.

S24. scrap. n.
1. fragment, particle, bit
2. waste, remnant,
rubbish, junk.

S25. scrumptious.
adj. delicious, tasty,
mouth-watering.

S26. scrutiny. n.
attention, examination,
investigation.

S27. scum. n.
1. trash, dregs, riffraff
2. film, foam, froth

S28. scuttle. v.
1. scurry, scamper, hurry
2. sink.

S29. seal. n.
1. emblem, symbol,
mark 2. fastener
v. 1. endorse, sign, stamp
2. close, fasten, secure

S30. search. v.
hunt, seek, scour,
explore, comb, ransack.

S31. secluded. adj.
isolated, remote,
sheltered, out-of-the-way.
A: accessible.

S32. secret. adj.
hidden, concealed,
private, confidential.
A: open, revealed.

S33. secure. adj.
1. protected, defended
2. unthreatened 3. sure,
certain, guaranteed
(secure future).
A: 1. insecure 2. unsafe
3. uncertain.

S34. sedate. adj.
calm, composed,
dignified, solemn.
A: nervous, excited.

S35. seduce. v. lure,
entice, tempt, snare
(seductive).

S36. seep. v. leak,
ooze, trickle, drip.

S37. segment. n.
portion, section, part,
piece.

S38. seize. v.
1. capture, arrest
2. grasp, grip, grab
3. confiscate. A: 1. free
2. loose, let go.

S39. seldom. adj.
rarely, not often.
A: often.

S40. select. v.
choose, pick, elect,
decide. (selection).

S41. sensible. adj.
wise, level-headed,
careful, thoughtful.

S42. sensitive. adj.
1. perceptive, responsive
2. touchy, irritable
3. sore, painful (injury
still sensitive).
A: 1. obtuse
2. thick-skinned.

S43. sentiment. n.
emotion, feeling,
attitude, opinion.

S44. sequel. n.
continuation, follow-up,
result, offshoot.

S45. sequence. n.
order, series,
progression.

S46. serious. adj.
1. solemn, grave,
sombre
2. earnest, sincere,
determined
3. important, critical,
significant (serious
matter).
A: 1. carefree, jolly
2. indifferent
3. trivial.

S

S47. set. v.
1. position, put, arrange (set in place) 2. harden, solidify 3. fix, define, establish (set limits) 4. located (set in) n. group, collection.

S48. settle. v.
1. immigrate, inhabit, live 2. resolve, work out, agree (settle matters) 3. pay, clear (settle debts) 4. decide, choose, fix (settle on) 5. land on, alight, rest (bird settled on branch).
A: 1. roam 2. confuse 4. disagree 5. rise.

S49. several. adj.
1. some, a few 2. separate, distinct (several opinions).

S50. severe. adj.
1. dangerous, critical, serious (severe illness) 2. stern, strict, forbidding (severe manner) 3. wild, stormy, biting (severe weather) A: 2. lenient, easy-going 3. mild.

S51. shabby. adj. worn, frayed, ragged, scruffy.

S52. shady. adj. dark, dim, shadowy, cool A: sunny, bright. (shade).

S53. shake. v. 1. wave, brandish, wag 2. vibrate, tremble, quiver, sway.

S54. sheer. adj.
1. transparent, fine, filmy 2. total, utter, complete (sheer nonsense) 3. vertical, precipitous, steep. A: 1. opaque 2. partial 3. sloping. H: shear.

S55. shift. v.
move, switch, exchange, transfer.

S56. shine. v. radiate, gleam, glow, illuminate. A: dim, darken.

S57. shock. n.
1. impact, jolt, blow 2. surprise, scare, trauma.

S58. shove. v.
push, jostle, nudge, jog.

S59. shrewd. adj.
1. astute, sharp,
discerning 2. sly, crafty,
wily. A: 1. ignorant,
unperceptive
2. straightforward.

S60. shrink. v.
1. shrivel, shorten,
contract 2. cower,
cringe, recoil.
A: 1. stretch 2. confront.

S61. shrivel. v. dry up,
wither, wilt, wrinkle.

S62. shun. v. avoid,
dodge, ignore, spurn.
A: welcome, seek.

S63. shut. v.
1. close, fasten, lock
2. enclose, confine,
imprison (shut in) 3. ban,
bar, exclude (shut out).
A: 1. open
2. release 3. admit.

S64. shy. adj. nervous,
reserved, modest, self-
conscious, timid. A: bold.

S65. side. n.
1. surface, face
2. edge, boundary,
perimeter (side of the
road) 3. team, group.

S66. sign. n.
1. symbol, token, mark
2. gesture, cue, signal
3. placard, billboard,
poster.

S67. silent. adj.
soundless, noiseless,
mute, quiet. A: noisy,
talkative. (silence).

S68. similar. adj.
alike, resembling,
equivalent, comparable.
A: different. (similarity).

S69. simple. adj.
1. easy, understandable,
uncomplicated
2. plain, undecorated
3. naive, unworldly,
dense. (simply, simplicity).

S

S70. sincere. adj.
honest, genuine, truthful, earnest.
A: deceitful. (sincerity).

S71. sinister. adj.
threatening, menacing, evil, ominous.
A: encouraging, kindly.

S72. situation. n.
1. place, position, location
2. circumstances, position, condition.

S73. size. n.
dimensions, extent, capacity, amount.

S74. skillful. adj.
expert, capable, trained, talented.
A: incompetent, clumsy. (skilled).

S75. skimp. v.
withhold, stint, scrimp, restrict. A: lavish.

S76. slack. adj.
loose, relaxed, limp.
A: tight, tense.

S77. slant. v.
incline, slope, lean, tilt.

S78. slap. n.
smack, hit, wallop.

S79. sleek. adj.
glossy, shiny, silky.

S80. slender. adj.
1. slim, lean, willowy
2. slight, faint, remote (slender chance).

S81. slight. adj.
1. frail, fragile, thin
2. small, tiny, insignificant. A: 1. husky
2. considerable.

S82. slink. v.
creep, skulk, steal, sidle.

S83. slope. n.
incline, hill, bank
v. slant, lean, tilt.

S84. slovenly. adj.
messy, untidy, dirty, disorderly, careless.
A: neat, clean, orderly.

S85. sluggish. adj.
slow, listless, inactive.
A: energetic.

S86. slumber. v. sleep, doze, snooze, nap.

S87. slump. v.
1. collapse, fall, drop, sag 2. decline, dip, fall off (sales slumped).
A: 2. improve.

S88. slur. v.
1. mumble, mutter
2. insult, defame, blacken. A: 1. enunciate
2. praise, laud.

S89. sly. adj. crafty, cunning, artful, sneaky.
A: open.

S90. small. adj.
1. little, tiny, petite
2. minor, trivial, unimportant (small details) 3. brief, concise, short. 4. meagre, stingy, inadequate (small helpings). A: 1. large, 2. major 3. lengthy 4. generous.

S91. smart. adj.
1. intelligent, clever, bright 2. chic, elegant, stylish. v. ache, sting, throb (wound smarts).

S92. smash. v. shatter, crush, break.

S93. smear. v.
1. rub, spread, daub
2. mar, tarnish, degrade (smear his reputation)
n. smudge, streak, stain.

S94. snag. n.
1. difficulty, obstacle, hindrance
2. concealed log, stump.

S95. snatch. v. grab, seize, pluck, clutch.

S96. snip. v. clip, cut, trim, lop. (snippet: small piece snipped off).

S97. snub. v. ignore, shun, rebuff.

S98. snug. adj.
1. cozy, comfortable, homely, safe 2. tight, too small (snug fit).

S99. soar. v. fly, climb, rise, mount.

S

S100. social. adj.
1. friendly, outgoing, neighbourly
2. communal, collective
A: antisocial.

S101. soft. adj.
1. pliable, supple, floppy
2. silky, furry, comfortable
3. low, gentle, muted (soft music) A: 1. hard
2. harsh 3. blaring.

S102. solace. n.
comfort, reassurance, support. A: distress.

S103. solemn. adj.
1. grave, serious, earnest
2. sombre, formal, ceremonial.
A: 1. jovial 2. informal.

S104. solitary. adj.
1. alone, lonely, separate
2. isolated, remote, secluded. A: 1. sociable
2. busy, central.

S105. solve. v.
work out, explain, decode, unravel.

S106. soothe. v.
pacify, calm, comfort, ease. A: rouse; irritate.

S107. sorry. adj.
1. regretful, repentant, apologetic
2. sad, unhappy.

A: 1. unrepentant
2. cheerful.

S108. sort. n.
type, make, brand, kind, species, group.

S109. sour. adj.
1. tart, acid, sharp, tangy
2. rancid, curdled, fermented 3. unpleasant, waspish, crabby (sour temper).
A: 1. sweet 2. fresh
3. good-humoured.

S110. source. n.
origin, beginning, cause.
A: result, end.

S111. space. n.
1. room, scope, range (need space) 2. gap, distance, span (empty space) 3. sky, stratosphere, universe.

S112. span. n.
1. distance, dimensions, scope, extent 2. arch.

S113. spare. v.
1. free, pardon, reprieve (spare the prisoner)
2. afford, manage, give (spare some time)
adj. extra, additional, surplus (spare parts).
A: 1. condemn.

S114. sparkle. v.
flash, glitter, shine, gleam.

S115. special. adj.
1. certain, specific, distinct. 2. unusual, uncommon, rare.

S116. specific. adj.
precise, exact, definite, defined.
A: approximate, vague

S117. speck. n.
particle, trace, grain, fleck, dot.

S118. spell. n.
1. interval, period, phase (brief spell of time)
2. charm, enchantment, magic.

S119. sphere. n.
globe, ball, orb.

S120. spill. v.
overflow, slop, slosh, drip, pour.

S121. spiral. n. helix, coil, whorl, corkscrew.

S122. spite. n. malice, ill will, hatred, hostility.
A: kindness. (spiteful).

S123. splendid. adj.
magnificent, imposing, sumptuous, grand.

S124. spoil. v. 1. ruin, mar, damage, bungle
2. decay, rot 3. indulge, pamper. A: 1. improve
2. preserve 3. discipline.

S125. spontaneous.
adj. impulsive, unplanned, instinctive.
A: contrived, calculated.

S126. spread. v.
1. unfold, extend, open (spread the cloth)
2. scatter, strew, disperse (spread her toys)
3. publish, circulate, repeat (spread the news).

S

S127. sprinkle. v.
scatter, dust, spatter,
spray.

S128. sprint. v. run,
dash, race. A: stroll.

S129. spurt. v.
spout, jet, gush, shoot.
A: drip, ooze.

S130. squabble. v.
quarrel, bicker, argue,
differ. A: agree.

S131. squalid. adj.
filthy, foul, impoverished,
ramshackle, dirty.
(squalor).

S132. squander. v.
waste, fritter, misuse.
A: save.

S133. squash. v.
1. crush, flatten, press,
squeeze 2. suppress,
overthrow, quell (squash
the uprising).

S134. squeamish. adj.
fussy, prudish, easily
shocked, weak-stomached.
A: brazen; tough.

S135. squirm. v.
wriggle, contort, twist,
writhe.

S136. stable. adj.
1. secure, immovable,
sound 2. enduring,
steadfast, continuing.

S137. stage. n.
1. platform 2. phase,
period 3. setting, scene.

S138. stagger. v.
stumble, reel, totter,
lurch.

S139. stamina. n.
endurance, strength,
vigour, energy.

S140. stamp. v.
1. stomp, tread, trample
2. brand, mark, print.

S141. stare. v. gaze,
gape, study, watch.

S142. startle. v.
frighten, surprise, scare,
alarm.

S143. status. n.
position, rank, class,
standing.

S144. stay. v.
1. remain, continue,
carry on, endure, wait
2. live, dwell, lodge, visit.
A: leave, go, quit.

S145. steal. v. rob,
thieve, burgle, loot.

S146. steep. adj.
sheer, vertical, abrupt,
precipitous.
A: flat, gradual.

S147. steer. v.
guide, control, pilot,
drive, navigate, lead.

S148. sterile. adj.
1. barren, infertile
2. disinfected,
uninfected, pure.

S149. still. adj.
1. motionless, unmoving,
immobile 2. calm, silent,
peaceful. adv. yet,
even now.

S150. stipulate. v.
specify, state, insist
upon, fix, guarantee.

S151. stir. v. 1. beat,
mix, whisk 2. move, act,
hasten (stir yourself)
3. rouse, excite, energise
(stir to action).

S152. stocky. adj.
thickset, sturdy, chunky,
squat.

S153. stow. v. store,
pack, load, deposit.

S154. strange. adj.
odd, unusual, abnormal,
bizarre.
A: normal, ordinary.

S155. strategy. n.
plan, scheme, policy,
tactics.

S156. stray. v. get lost,
wander, straggle, roam.

S157. strength. n.
1. energy, force, might,
power 2. number, size
(strength of the army).

S158. strict. adj. stern,
severe, firm, rigid.
A: lenient.

S159. stride. v.
march, pace.

S160. stroll. v.
saunter, promenade,
walk, amble, wander.
A: hurry.

S161. struggle. v.
1. strain, strive, labour
2. battle, fight, grapple.

S

S162. stubborn. adj. obstinate, wilful, immovable, dogged.

S163. stun. v. 1. daze, stupefy, knock out 2. amaze, astound, shock.

S164. stupid. adj. 1. dense, simple, slow 2. foolish, idiotic, inane, senseless. A: wise, thoughtful.

S165. style. n. fashion, trend, mode, method.

S166. subject. n. topic, theme, matter.

S167. submit. v. 1. surrender, give in, yield 2. offer, present, hand in.

S168. subsequent. adj. next, following, later, succeeding.

S169. subside. v. 1. settle, sink 2. abate, ebb, lessen, decrease.

S170. substantial. adj. big, sizable, considerable, large.

S171. succeed. v. achieve, attain, complete, win. A: fail. (success, successful).

S172. sudden. adj. abrupt, hasty, unexpected, hurried. A: gradual, expected. (suddenly).

S173. suffering. n. sorrow, distress, misery, ordeal.

S174. suggest. v. 1. propose, recommend, advise 2. hint, imply, indicate.

S175. suitable. adj. apt, fitting, proper, relevant. A: unsuitable.

S176. sullen. adj. sulky, gloomy, grumpy.

S177. superb. adj. excellent, splendid, superior.

S178. supervise. v. oversee, manage, direct, control. (supervisor, supervision).

S179. supple. adj. flexible, bendable, pliant.

S180. supply. v. give, provide, equip, furnish.

S181. suppose. v. assume, presume, guess, imagine.

S182. sure. adj.
1. confident, certain, convinced, positive
2. reliable, dependable, loyal (a sure friend).
A: 1. uncertain
2. wavering.

S183. surprise. n. shock, bombshell, wonder, amazement.

S184. surround. v. encircle, enclose.

S185. suspicion. n. distrust, doubt, misgiving, feeling, hunch.
A: trust, certainty.

S186. swap. v. trade, exchange, barter.

S187. swarm. n. horde, host, pack, mob, throng.

S188. swell. v.
1. puff, bloat, distend, bulge
2. billow, surge, intensify.
A: 1. shrink, compress
2. lessen, wane (swollen).

S189. swindle. v. cheat, defraud, con, trick.

S190. symbol. n. sign, emblem, badge, token. (symbolise).

S191. sympathy. n.
1. understanding, rapport, affinity
2. concern, compassion.
A: 1. hostility
2. indifference.
(sympathise, sympathetic)

S192. symptom. n. sign, indication, warning, evidence.

S193. system. n. process, method, order, structure.

T

T1. table. n. 1. list, chart, index, schedule 2. plateau, flatland, plain 3. teatable, desk.

T2. taboo. adj. forbidden, banned, prohibited. A: allowed.

T3. taciturn. adj. reserved, untalkative, silent. A: talkative.

T4. tackle. n. 1. gear, kit, equipment, tools 2. rig, hoist, pulley v. attempt, try, undertake. A: v. evade.

T5. tactful. adj. considerate, discreet, polite, diplomatic. A: tactless. (tact).

T6. take. v. 1. get, obtain, acquire 2. seize, grab, snatch 3. deliver, bring, lead, transport 4. happen, occur (take place). A: lose 2. give, loose 3. fetch.

T7. tall. adj. high, lofty, towering, lanky. A: short.

T8. tame. adj. 1. domesticated, broken, gentle, docile 2. dull, boring, unexciting. A: 1. wild 2. exciting.

T9. tangible. adj. touchable, solid, material, real. A: intangible, ethereal.

T10. target. n. object, goal, aim, mark, point.

T11. tariff. n. rate, fee, price, cost.

T12. task. n. job, duty, work, errand, mission, assignment.

T13. tasteful. adj. attractive, aesthetic, elegant, fitting. A: tasteless. (taste).

T14. tasty. adj. flavourful, delicious, appetising, delectable. A: bland.

T15. **taunt.** v. jeer, insult, mock, ridicule. A: flatter.

T16. **tax.** n. tariff, duty, custom, toll.

T17. **team.** n. group, crew, company, band, gang. H: teem.

T18. **tear.** v. 1. rip, split, rend, snag 2. speed, race, rush, sprint. A: 1. mend 2. stroll H: tear.

T19. **tedious.** adj. boring, dull, tiring, drawn-out. A: interesting. stimulating.

T20. **teem.** v. swarm, overflow, abound, over-crowd (teem with) H: team.

T21. **tell.** v. 1. recount, relate, describe, explain 2. distinguish, identify, recognise (tell them apart) 3. instruct, direct, order (tell them to stop). A: listen.

T22. temperament. n. nature, personality, disposition, character.

T23. temporary. adj. passing, brief, impermanent, fleeting. A: permanent.

T24. tempt. v. entice, lure, attract, seduce.

T25. tend. v. 1. be likely, apt, be disposed to 2. care for, wait on, keep, protect.

T26. tender. adj. 1. sore, sensitive, painful 2. compassionate, gentle, kind 3. young, immature, inexperienced (tender age). A: 2. hard, pitiless 3. mature, worldly. (tenderness, tenderly).

T27. tense. adj. 1. taut, tight, stiff 2. strained, uneasy, anxious. A: 1. slack 2. relaxed, calm. (tension) H: tents.

T

T28. tenuous. adj.
weak, flimsy,
insubstantial, indefinite.
A: strong, substantial.

T29. term. n. 1. word,
phrase, expression
2. span, period, session
3. condition, clause,
demand (terms of the
contract).

T30. terminate. v.
end, finish, stop, close.
A: begin, open.
(termination).

T31. terror. n.
fear, dread, horror, awe.
A: reassurance.

T32. terse. adj. brief,
crisp, concise, curt.
A: long-winded.

T33. test. n.
1. exam, quiz, check-up
2. trial, dry-run, attempt.

T34. texture. n.
feel, weave, structure.

T35. thaw. v.
melt, dissolve, liquefy,
unfreeze.
A: freeze, solidify.

T36. theme. n. subject,
topic, focus, motif,
melody.

T37. theory. n.
1. principle, law, science
2. assumption,
explanation, idea,
concept.

T38. therapy. n.
treatment, healing,
remedy.

T39. therefore. adv.
consequently, hence,
thus, accordingly, so.

T40. thick. adj.
1. deep, wide, bulky
2. stupid, dull, slow
3. congealed, clotted,
viscous (thick sauce)
4. dense (thick smoke)
5. swarming, teeming,
crowded (train thick with
passengers).
A: 1. thin 2. smart
3. runny 4. empty.

T41. thin. adj.
1. lean, slender, skinny
2. delicate, sheer, fragile
3. watery, runny, diluted (thin gravy)
4. weak, inadequate (thin excuse).
A: 1,2. coarse
3. thick 4. adequate.

PRISON CANTEEN
TOO MUCH WATER!

T42. thorough. adj.
1. painstaking, careful, complete (thorough overhaul)
2. total, downright, utter (thorough nuisance)
A: 1. careless 2. partial.

T43. threat. n.
1. warning, caution, omen
2. menace, danger, risk. (threaten, threatening).

T44. thrilling. adj.
exciting, stirring, electrifying.
A: boring, tedious. (thrill).

T45. thrive. v. flourish, grow, prosper, succeed.
A: wither, fail.

T46. throb. v.
beat, pulsate, pound.

T47. through. adj.
1. finished, done, ended (work was through for the day) 2. direct (through train) 3. during (through the concert) adv. into and out of, beyond, between.

T48. thrust. v. 1. push, shove, propel, force
2. stab, lunge, pierce.
A: 1. pull 2. parry.

T49. thug. n. mugger, terrorist, gangster, hoodlum, vandal.

T50. thwart. v. out-manoeuvre, foil, stop, obstruct. A: help.

T51. ticket. n. coupon, voucher, pass.

T52. tidbit. n. morsel, mouthful, choice bit.

T53. tidy. adj. 1. neat, smart, presentable (person) 2. orderly, organised, immaculate (place). A: 1. unkempt 2. messy.

T

T54. tie. v.
1. bind, fasten, knot
2. attach, join, link
3. confine, restrict, limit (tied to the home)
4. draw (the teams tied).
A: 1,2. untie 3. free.

T55. tier. n. row, rank, level, layer, store. H: tear.

T56. tight. adj.
1. firm, secure, fixed
2. taut, tense, stretched (tight rope) 3. pinched, cramped, snug (tight fit)
A: 1. loose 2. slack 3. empty.

T57. tilt. v. slant, lean, slope, incline, tip.

T58. timid. adj. fearful, shy, nervous.
A: bold, brave.

T59. tinge. v. colour, dye, stain
n. tint, shade, hue.

T60. tip. v. tilt, lean, topple, overturn
n. 1. point, top

2. summit, apex, peak.
3. hint, clue, advice
4. small reward, gratuity.

T61. tired. adj.
1. weary, exhausted, fatigued 2. sleepy, drowsy. A: 1. refreshed. (tire, tiresome).

T62. title. n.
1. heading, name, inscription
2. rank, position, status.

T63. toil. n. hard work, drudgery, labour
v. work, slog, slave.

T64. tolerant. adj. understanding, forgiving, softhearted, open-minded.
A: prejudiced, strict.

T65. tone. n. 1. pitch, sound, expression
2. shade, tint, hue
3. atmosphere, mood, manner.

T66. tool. n. instrument, implement, utensil, device.

T67. top. n. 1. apex, summit, upper surface, crown 2. lid, cover, cap 3. highest position, head, lead.
A: 1, 2. bottom, base 3. rear.

T68. topic. n.
subject, theme, matter.

T69. topple. v.
tip, upset, overturn.

T70. torment. v.
1. annoy, pester, harass 2. torture, persecute, bully n. suffering, agony, pain, distress.
A: 1, 2 please, delight, comfort.

T71. torn. adj.
ripped, rent, split.

T72. torrent. n.
cascade, downpour, outburst, deluge.

T73. total. n.
sum, whole, amount adj. complete, utter, absolute, entire.
A: adj. partial. (totally).

T74. touching. adj.
1. moving, emotional, affecting, sentimental 2. meeting, converging, tangent.

T75. tour. n.
trip, excursion, journey.

T76. tow. v.
haul, drag, pull, trail.
A: push H: toe.

T77. toxic. adj.
poisonous, noxious, deadly, lethal.

T78. trace. n.
1. tinge, touch, bit 2. sign, mark, evidence v. track, trail, follow.

T79. tradition. n.
custom, convention, folklore. (traditional).

T80. tragedy. n.
disaster, calamity, misfortune. A: blessing.

T81. trait. n.
characteristic, feature, quality.

T

T82. tranquil. adj.
peaceful, serene, restful,
undisturbed.
A: troubled, agitated.

T83. transfer. v.
move, remove, relocate,
shift, transport.

T84. transmit. v.
1. broadcast
2. send, deliver, pass on.

T85. transpire. v.
1. happen, occur, take
place 2. come to light.

T86. trap. n.
1. snare, pitfall 2. trick,
ploy, wile v. catch, snare,
capture, corner.

T87. trash. n.
1. rubbish, junk, garbage
2. nonsense, drivel (don't
talk trash). A: treasure.

T88. travel. v. journey,
voyage, tour, wander.

T89. traverse. v.
cross, go over.

T90. travesty. n.
1. mockery, satire,
lampoon 2. distortion,
misrepresentation.

T91. tremendous. adj.
1. huge, immense,
enormous 2. dreadful,
alarming, fearsome
(tremendous shock).
A: 1. tiny.

T92. tremor. n.
shaking, vibration,
shudder.

T93. trend. n.
1. fashion, style (latest
trend) 2. tendency,
direction, swing (trend
towards).

T94. trespass. v.
intrude, invade, violate.

T95. tribute. n.
1. praise, recognition,
compliment.

T96. trickle. v. dribble,
drip, leak, seep. A: gush.

T97. trim. v. 1. prune, clip, shear. 2. decorate, garnish, embellish.

T98. trip. n. journey, voyage, outing. v. stumble, stagger, slip.

T99. trite. adj. corny, unoriginal, banal. A: original, unusual.

T100. triumph. n. victory, success, achievement. A: failure, defeat.

T101. trivial. adj. unimportant, trite insignificant, frivolous, A: weighty, important.

T102. trophy. n. 1. award, cup, medal, prize 2. loot, booty, souvenir.

T103. tropical. adj. sultry, humid, muggy, torrid. Trophy and tropical come from the same Greek word that means 'a turn': 'turning back' the enemy and 'the turning' of the sun.

T104. trustworthy. adj. responsible, reliable, honest, dependable. A: unreliable, corrupt (trust trusting).

T105. truthful. adj. honest, accurate, frank, sincere, undeceitful. A: untruthful, deceitful.

T106. try. v. 1. attempt, endeavour, aim 2. test, sample (try this cake) 3. risk, venture, undertake (don't try that) 4. annoy, tire, drain (Tom tried her patience).

T107. tuft. n. 1. clump, bunch, wisp 2. crest, plume, topknot.

T

T108. tug. v.
yank, pull, jerk, tow.

T109. tumult. n.
uproar, commotion, din, hullabaloo.
A: peace, calm.

T110. turmoil. n.
chaos, confusion, upheaval, disorder.
A: order.

T111. turn. 1. revolve, rotate, spin 2. change, alter, transform, become (milk turns into cheese) 3. arrive, appear (turn up) 4. refuse, decline, reject (turn down) 5. eject, evict, transpire (turn out).

T112. twinge. n. ache, spasm, throb, pang.

T113. twinkle. v. glimmer, glisten, flicker, sparkle.

T114. twist. v. 1. coil, spiral, curl 2. entwine, weave, wind 3. wriggle, squirm 4. warp, pervert, colour (twist the truth) 5. wrench, wrest, yank (twist the lid).
A: 1, 2. straighten, unravel.

T115. twitch. v. fidget, jerk, jump, squirm.

T116. tycoon. n. wealthy businessman, magnate, financier.

T117. type. n. 1. kind, sort, variety, species, category 2. typeface.

T118. typical. adj. average, representative, usual, characteristic.
A: unusual.

T119. tyranny. n.
1. cruelty, harshness
2. unjust rule, dictatorship
A: 1. fairness
2. democracy (tyrant, tyrannical).

U1. ugly. adj.
unsightly, hideous,
grotesque, repulsive.

U2. ulterior. adj.
hidden, unexpressed,
undisclosed, selfish.
A: obvious.

U3. ultimate. adj.
1. final, concluding,
eventual (ultimate goal)
2. maximum, highest,
greatest (ultimate
reward). A: 1. initial
2. least. (ultimately).

U4. umpire. n.
judge, referee,
adjudicator, decider.

U5. unassuming. adj.
modest, simple,
informal, natural.

U6. unaware. adj.
ignorant, unsuspecting,
oblivious, unknowing.
A: aware. (unawares).

U7. unbalanced. adj.
1. uneven, unequal,
lopsided, unstable
2. deranged, insane, mad.

U8. unbiased. adj.
impartial, just, neutral,
tolerant. A: prejudiced.

U9. uncanny. adj.
extraordinary,
remarkable, mysterious,
supernatural.

U10. uncertain. adj.
unsure, doubtful,
indefinite.

U11. uncompromising.
adj. rigid, inflexible,
strict, firm.

U12. unconscious.
adj. 1. senseless
2. unaware, insensitive
3. automatic, reflex,
instinctive (unconscious
action).

U13. uncouth. adj.
crude, coarse, rough,
loutish. A: refined.

U14. undercurrent. n.
1. undertow, riptide
2. hidden feeling, mood,
atmosphere, vibrations.

U15. undergo. v.
experience, bear, endure,
suffer. A: evade, escape.

U16. underhand. adj.
unethical, devious,
sneaky, dishonest.
A: open, honest.

U

U17. undermine. v.
1. dig under, wear away
2. destroy, ruin, weaken (undermine his position).

U18. understand. v.
1. comprehend, apprehend, realise
2. hear, learn, presume.

U19. undertake. v.
1. take on, set about, assume
2. agree to, promise.
A: 1. abandon 2. decline.

U20. undo. v.
1. detach, disconnect, untie
2. overturn, ruin, cancel (undo his good work).
A: 1. tie, fasten
2. help.

U21. unfit. adj.
unsuitable, unprepared, incapable.

U22. ungainly. adj.
ungraceful, clumsy, awkward.
A: graceful, lithe.

U23. unidentified. adj.
nameless, unknown, unrecognised, mysterious, obscure.

U24. unique. adj.
single, rare, exceptional, matchless. A: ordinary.

U25. unit. n.
1. measure, quantity
2. section, module, item, component, detachment.

U26. unite. v. join, combine, merge, co-operate, bond. A: divide, separate. (united, unity).

U27. unkempt. adj.
dishevelled, rumpled, tousled, untidy, scruffy.

U28. unkind. adj.
unfeeling, nasty, cruel, spiteful. A: kind.

U29. unlimited. adj.
1. unrestricted
2. boundless, endless, infinite.
A: 1. partial, controlled
2. limited.

U30. unobtrusive. adj.
inconspicuous, modest, reserved, unassertive.

U31. unpleasant. adj.
nasty, disgusting, offensive, upsetting.
A: pleasant.

U32. unpredictable.
adj. uncertain, erratic, changeable, unexpected.

U33. unruly. adj.
unmanageable, wild, beyond control, headstrong.

U34. unsafe. adj. dangerous, risky, exposed, insecure. A: safe, secure.

U35. unscrupulous. adj. dishonest, amoral, devious, shameless, corrupt. A: honourable.

U36. unstable. adj. 1. unsteady, wobbly, shaky 2. changeable, inconsistent, volatile (unstable personality).

U37. untidy. adj. messy, disorganised, sloppy, scruffy.

U38. upheaval. n. violent change, disruption, chaos, turmoil.

U39. upper. adj. topmost, above, superior.

U40. upright. adj. 1. vertical, erect 2. honest, trustworthy, just, good. A: 1. horizontal, prone 2. crooked.

U41. uproarious. adj. 1. riotous, confused, excited, noisy 2. hilarious, hysterical. A: 1. tranquil 2. solemn.

U42. upset. v. 1. overturn, topple 2. distress, annoy, anger. A: 1. right 2. comfort, please.

U43. upshot. n. result, outcome, effect, end.

U44. urban. adj. city, civic, metropolitan. A: rural.

U45. urge. v. 1. force, goad, push, drive 2. persuade, rouse, advise, implore.

U46. useful. adj. helpful, advantageous, practical, functional. A: useless.

U47. usual. adj. customary, habitual, traditional, common.

U48. utilise. v. use.

U49. utter. v. speak, say, tell adj. complete, total, absolute. (utterly).

V

V1. vacant. adj.
1. unoccupied, empty, unfilled, uninhabited
2. blank, expressionless (vacant stare).

V2. vagrant. n. tramp, beggar, hobo, wanderer.

V3. vague. adj. indefinite, unclear, indistinct, veiled.
A: clear.

V4. vain. adj. 1. proud, conceited, self-admiring
2. useless, futile, ineffective (vain attempt).
A: 1. modest, humble
2. successful.

V5. valid. adj.
1. suitable, convincing, effective 2. legal, official.

V6. value. n. worth, merit, importance. (valuable).

V7. vandal. n. hooligan, looter, wrecker, raider.

V8. vanish. v. disappear, dematerialise, fade, go.

V9. vanity. n. pride, conceit, arrogance.

V10. variety. n.
1. change, diversity, contrast 2. mixture, assortment, jumble
3. kind, type, species (which variety?).

V11. vary. v.
1. change, alter, adapt
2. differ, contrast, disagree.

V12. vast. adj.
1. wide, broad, immense
2. boundless, endless, immeasurable.
A: 1. narrow 2. limited.

V13. vault. n. 1. dome, arch, arched ceiling
2. cellar, crypt, strongroom v. jump over, hurdle, leap.

V14. veer. v. swerve, turn, dodge, wheel.

V15. vehement. adj. intense, passionate, fierce, excited.
A: indifferent. (vehemently).

V16. veil. n.
1. cloak, screen, cover
2. scarf, yashmak, purdah
3. v. conceal, cover.

V17. velocity. n. speed.

V18. veneer. n. facing, facade, outerlayer.

V19. vengeance. n. revenge, retaliation. (vengeful).

V20. ventilate. v. air, oxygenate, air-condition, cool.

V21. venture. v. try, risk, attempt, dare n. project, enterprise, gamble. (venturesome).

V22. verdict. n. judgment, finding, decision.

V23. verge. n. edge, border, margin, rim.

V24. verify. v. confirm, prove, sustain, show. A: disprove, falsify.

V25. versatile. adj. adaptable, talented, ingenious, multipurpose.

V26. version. n. account, story, interpretation, translation.

V27. very. adv. extremely, greatly, most, truly, especially.

V28. vessel. n. 1. ship, boat, craft 2. container, receptacle, pot, jug.

V29. viable. adj. work-able, usable, practical.

V30. vice. n.
1. corruption, sin wickedness, immorality,
2. failing, weakness, shortcoming (his vice is gossiping).

V31. vicious. adj.
1. brutal, ruthless, cruel (vicious attack) 2. savage, fierce, dangerous (vicious animal) 3. spiteful, malicious, scandalous (vicious rumour).
A: 1. compassionate
2. tame, playful
3. complimentary.

V32. vigorous. adj. energetic, active, forceful, dynamic.
A: lethargic. (vigour).

V33. vile. adj. disgusting, offensive, loathsome, sordid.
A: good, admirable.

V34. vindictive. adj. unforgiving, spiteful, malicious. A: forgiving.

V35. violent. adj.
1. severe, powerful, fierce (violent storm)
2. brutal, savage, ferocious (violent attack)
3. passionate, uncontrollable, explosive (violent temper).
A: 1. mild 2. gentle
3. composed.

V

V36. visible. adj.
seeable, discernible,
clear, distinct, noticeable
(visibility).

V37. vision. n.
1. sight, perception
2. imagination, concept,
plan 3. fantasy, dream,
hallucination
4. ghost, apparition.

V38. vista. n.
scenery, view, landscape.

V39. vitality. n.
strength, life-force,
energy, vigour.
A: torpor. (vital).

V40. vivacious. adj.
lively, animated, bubbly,
jolly. A: languid, dull.

V41. vivid. adj.
1. bright, intense,
brilliant, colourful
2. realistic, lifelike,
dramatic (vivid dream).
A: 1. dull, drab.

V42. vocation. n.
career, profession, job,
trade.

V43. void. adj.
1. empty, blank, bare
2. invalid, not legally
binding (null and void).

V44. voluntary. adj.
optional, unforced.

A: compulsory.
(volunteer, voluntarily).

V45. vow. n. promise,
pledge, oath.

V46. vulgar. adj.
coarse, common, rude,
obscene.
A: refined. (vulgarity).

V47. vulnerable. adj.
defenceless, unprotected,
easily hurt, sensitive.
A: protected, thick-
skinned.

W

W1. wade. v. walk in
water, ford, trudge.

W2. wage. n. salary,
payment, earnings
v. carry on, practice
(wage war).

W3. wager. v.
bet, gamble, stake.

W4. wail. v.
cry, moan, howl, whine.

W5. wait. v. 1. remain, linger, stay 2. hesitate, delay, pause. H: weight.

W6 wake. v.
1. awaken, rouse.
A: sleep.

W7. wallow. v.
1. flounder, tumble, roll (in mud) 2. luxuriate, revel, bask (in luxury).

W8. wan. adj.
pale, sickly, pasty.
A: flushed. H: won.

W9. wander. v.
1. meander, ramble, roam, rove
2. drift, veer, swerve (wander off course).

W10. wane. v.
fade, lessen, decrease, weaken.
A: wax, increase.

W11. want. v.
1. need, lack, require
2. desire, crave, fancy.
A: have, reject.

W12. ward. n.
1. hospital ward
2. voting district, zone
v. fend off, repel, deflect.

W13. warm. adj.
1. lukewarm, tepid (warm water) 2. sunny, bright, sultry (warm weather) 3. loving, kind, friendly (warm nature).
A: 1. hot, cold 2. dull 3. aloof.

W14. warning. n.
alarm, signal, omen, advice. (warn).

W15. warp. v. bend, twist, distort, deform, buckle. A: straighten.

W16. wary. adj.cautious, alert, watchful suspicious,
A: unwary, rash.

W17. wash. v. clean, cleanse, bathe, scrub, launder.

W18. waste. n.
rubbish, garbage, junk
v. misuse, fritter, squander. A: v. save, conserve. H: waist.

W19. watch. v.
1. look at, stare, regard, notice 2. pay attention, be careful (watch your step) 3. guard, tend, mind (watch the sheep). (watchful).

W20. wave. v.
1. flutter, swing, shake, signal n. 1. swell, billow, breaker 2. pulse, vibration (radio waves) 3. curl, kink, curve (hair waves).

W21. way. n. 1. route, path, course 2. method, procedure, system 3. manner, habit, style.

W22. weak. adj.
1. frail, feeble, delicate 2. fragile, breakable, flimsy 3. powerless, ineffectual. A: 1. robust, hardy 2. substantial 3. forceful. H: week. (weaken, weakness).

W23. wealth. n.
1. riches, fortune, assets 2. affluence, prosperity, luxury 3. abundance, quantity (wealth of detail). A: poverty, want.

W24. weary. adj.
tired, exhausted, drowsy, bored.
A: refreshed, interested.

W25. weight. n.
1. heaviness, mass
2. burden, load, strain.
H: wait.

W26. weird. adj.
odd, bizarre, eerie, mysterious. A: normal.

W27. wet. adj.
moist, damp, soaking, clammy, sodden. A: dry.

W28. wheeze. v.
gasp, pant, puff.

W29. whim. n. notion, caprice, impulse, urge.

W30. whimper. v.
cry, moan, snivel.

W31. whine. v.
complain, grumble, cry, whimper.

W32. whole. adj.
complete, entire, total, intact. A: partial, incomplete. H: hole.

W33. wholesome. adj.
1. healthful, nutritious, hygienic
2. healthy, decent.
A: 1. unwholesome.

W34. wide. adj. broad, extensive, far-reaching, vast.
A: narrow, restricted.

W35. wield. v. flourish, wave, swing, manage. H: weald.

W36. wild. adj.
1. free, untamed, natural
2. waste, desolate, rugged (wild countryside)
3. unruly, rowdy, uncontrolled (wild behaviour). A: 1. tame
2. cultivated
3. disciplined.

W37. wilt. v. wither, droop, shrivel.

W38. wily. adj. devious, sly, crafty, tricky.
A: straightforward.

W39. win. v. 1. attain, achieve, succeed, triumph. A: lose.

W40. wise. adj. intelligent, shrewd, balanced, perceptive.
A: foolish.

W41. wish. v. hope, long, desire.

W42. wistful. adj.
1. longing, forlorn, sorrowful
2. dreamy, pensive, reflective.

W43. wit. n. humour, repartee, satire. (witty).

W44. withdraw. v.
1. retreat, go away, depart
2. remove, extract.
A: 1. arrive, stay.

W45. withhold. v.
1. keep back, retain
2. deny, suppress.
A: 1. grant
2. reveal.

W46. witness. n.
1. onlooker, observer, bystander
2. see, observe, attend
3. testify, endorse.

W47. woe. n. trouble, suffering, misery, grief.
A: joy, good fortune.

W48. wonder. v.
1. question, ponder
2. admire, marvel marvel, miracle, phenomenon.
A: 1. understand, ignore
2. accept.

W

W49. work. n.
1. effort, labour, exertion
2. employment, profession, trade
3. task, chore
4. creation, composition, performance, (work of art) v. 1. toil, labour
2. function, go, operate (how does this work?)
A: 1, 3. play
2. entertainment, unemployment.

W50. worn. adj.
1. frayed, threadbare, shabby, decrepit
2. exhausted, tired, fatigued. A: 1. new
2. refreshed.

W51. worry. n.
anxiety, unease, distress, apprehension.
A: assurance, trust.

W52. worth. n.
1. value, price
2. usefulness, benefit, importance.

W53. wrap. v. enclose, swathe, enfold, bundle, cover. A: unwrap, expose. H: rap.

W54. wrath. n.
anger, rage, fury, ire.

W55. wreck. v.
ruin, destroy, spoil
n. ruin, debris, remains.
A: v. build, save, salvage.

W56. wrench. v.
twist, wrest, jerk, force.

W57. wretched. adj.
1. despairing, heartbroken, depressed
2. despicable, vile, worthless. A: 1. happy, carefree 2. noble.

W58. wrong. adj.
1. incorrect, mistaken, untrue 2. dishonest, illegal, immoral 3. faulty, amiss, out of order (something's wrong).
A: 1. correct 2. ethical.

W59. wry. adj.
1. twisted, crooked, askew 2. ironic, cynical, sarcastic (wry comment).
A: straight, symmetrical.

X1. xenophobic. adj. fearing strangers, nationalistic, insular, narrow-minded.

X2. xerox. v. copy, reproduce, photostat.

X3. x-rated. adj. censored, classified.

X4. x-ray. n. radiogram.

X5. xylophone. n. marimba, vibra-harp.

Y

Y1. yank. v. tug, jerk, pull.

Y2. yap. v. yelp, bark.

Y3. yard. n. 1. measure 2. courtyard, compound, enclosure, garden.

Y4. yardstick. n. measure, ruler.

Y5. yarn. n. 1. thread, wool 2. tale, story, narrative.

Y6. yearn. v. long, crave, hanker, desire. A: hate. (yearning).

Y7. yell. v. shout, holler, bawl, bellow, scream.

Y8. yellow. adj. lemon, ochre, gold, mustard, saffron, buttercup.

Y9. yen. n. desire, longing, craving, fancy, wish. A: disinterest.

Y10. yes. adv. just so, true, surely, truly, certainly. A: no.

Y11. yield. v. 1. produce, bear, grow (yield fruit) 2. surrender, give in, submit (yield to force) 3. bend, sag, flex, bow (yield under the weight).

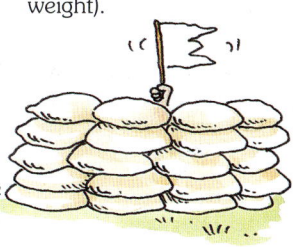

Y12. yoke. n. 1. harness, collar frame 2. pair, brace, couple 3. burden, strain, pressure (yoke of responsibility).

Z

Y13. yokel. n.
bumpkin, rustic, peasant.

Y14. yonder. adj. more
distant, further, remote.
A: nearby.

Y15. young. adj.
1. youthful, minor, junior
2. immature, childish,
babyish (young for his
age).

Y16. youth. n.
1. lad, boy 2. teenagers,
young people,
adolescents (youth of
today) 3. childhood,
schooldays, prime (time
of your youth).

Y17. yowl. v.
shriek, caterwaul, howl.

Z

Z1. zany. adj.
unconventional, crazy,
weird, comical. A: dull.

Z2. zeal. n. eagerness,
enthusiasm, energy.
A: lethargy, indifference.

Z3. zenith. n. highest
point, peak, finest, best.
A: nadir.

Z4. zephyr. n.
light breeze, puff.
A: gust, gale.

Z5. zero. n.
naught, nil, nothing.
A: infinity, everything.

Z6. zest. n.
relish, gusto, passion,
enthusiasm. A: apathy.

Z7. zip. n. energy, pep,
vim, vigour, vitality.
A: torpor.

Z8. zone. n. region,
district, area, quarter,
sector, locality.

Z9. zoo. n.
menagerie, vivarium.

Z10. zoom. v. dash,
hurtle, rush, whiz, race.